GROWING UP STRONG

Four
North Country
Women
Recall Their
Lives

GROWING UP STRONG

Four
North Country
Women
Recall Their
Lives

by
Sadie Cantin
Melba Wrisley
Marilyn Cross
Sonja Aubin

Edited by Joan Potter

Pinto Press
Elizabethtown, NY

Cover design and art by Alison Muñoz
Book design by Dale Schroeder, Synergistic Data Systems

Library of Congress Catalog Card Number: 95-68093

Publisher's Cataloging in Publication
(Prepared by Quality Books Inc.)

Growing up strong : four north country women recall their
lives / by Sadie Cantin ... [et al.]; edited by Joan Potter.
P. cm.
Preassigned LCCN-95-68093
ISBN O-9632476-2-X

1. Cantin, Sadie. 2. Wrisley, Melba. 3. Cross, Marilyn. 4. Aubin,
Sonia. 5. Adirondack Mountains (N.Y.)—History. 6. Adirondack
Mountains (N. Y.)—Social life and customs.

F127,A2G76 1995   974.7'504
                                     QBI95-20074

10 9 8 7 6 5 4 3 2 1

Published by

Pinto Press

Elizabethtown, NY

Acknowledgments

Thanks are due to an early supporter of the project, Essex County Historian Reid Larson, for his help in funding our workshops and organizing public readings of some of this material; to New Russia photographer Al Reiner for his sensitive portraits of the four writers; to Conrad Hutchins for sharing his collection of old photographs; to Jeffrey Fields for restoring some of the photos, and to the Elizabethtown Social Center for providing workshop space at Hale House.

Melba Wrisley wishes to thank the following people for providing her with information: Barbara Abel for her interview with Dr. Gersen, Anne Mackinnon for notes taken from her article in the April 1993 issue *of Adirondack Life* magazine, Roger Bartlett, John Elser, Logan Phinney, Jr., and Ross Carson.

Special appreciation goes to the Reverend Frederick Shaw of the United Church of Christ in Elizabethtown for providing space for our public readings and for agreeing to sponsor our grant request to the Essex County Arts Council.

Finally, this book was made possible, in part, with public funds from the New York State Council on the Arts Decentralization Program administered locally by the Essex County Arts Council.

Introduction

$\mathcal{E}$arly in June 1993, I sat at a table in the parish hall of the United Church of Christ in Elizabethtown, New York, with a group of older women and men who were gathered there to write about their lives. I had moved to this small community two and a half years before, and had spent part of my time there writing about the Adirondacks and teaching a memoir-writing workshop at a nearby state prison boot camp. Seeing the pleasure and pride the young prisoners expressed at being given the permission and encouragement to tell their life stories was a gratifying experience for me. I thought of organizing a similar workshop for a group of women and men who had been born and spent all their lives in two remote Adirondack villages—Elizabethtown and Lewis.

I'd earlier enjoyed meeting a woman named Sadie Cantin— 86 years old at the time—who was a terrific storyteller with a quirky sense of humor. She was my starting point. She said she'd be delighted to join the writing workshop and help me find other likely candidates.

The county historian, Reid Larson, became interested in the project and was successful in acquiring a grant from the Essex County Arts Council to help support the workshop. Ken White, then the director of the Elizabethtown Social Center, offered us a weekly meeting place.

But my early enthusiasm about the workshop was dampened rather quickly as, one by one, people stopped showing up. They were polite and apologetic, but they'd decided that for one reason or another they had been unrealistic about how much time they wanted to put into the hard task of writing.

After a few weeks, only four women remained: Sadie Cantin, Melba Wrisley, Marilyn Cross, and Sonja Aubin. But they turned out to be more wonderful than I could ever have hoped for. Not only were they enthusiastic, hardworking, and inventive, but they were eloquent writers. Their ages ranged from 57 to 86; each was born in a different decade, in different circumstances, and each had a distinctive voice. It has been a gift for me to be able to get to know these women through their remarkable writing and the many hours I've been privileged to spend with them.

This book is a collection of the work produced by these four women, arranged by the age of the writer and placed chronologically within each section. The text is interspersed with old photographs, many from the women's own collections.

It is my hope that the stories of the struggles and victories of these four writers will have special meaning to the women and men who share their memories and will offer inspiration to all readers.

— Joan Potter

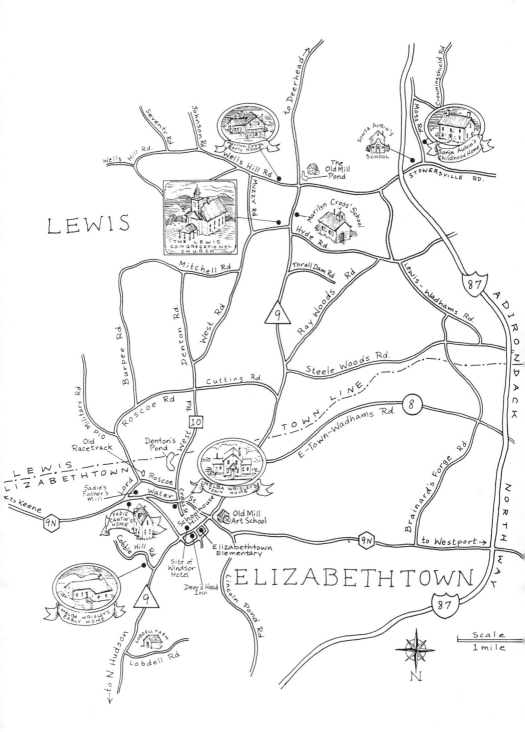

LEWIS

to Deerhead →

Seventy Rd.

Johnson Rd.

Wells Hill Rd

Wells Hill Rd.

Marilyn Cross' Early Home

The Old Mill Pond

Muzzy Rd

THE LEWIS CONGREGATIONAL CHURCH

Marilyn Cross' School

Hyde Rd.

Sonja Aubin's School

Moss Rd.

Crowninshield Rd.

Sonja Aubin's Childhood Home

STOWERSVILLE RD.

Mitchell Rd.

Thrall Dam Rd.

Ray Woods Rd.

Lewis-Wadhams Rd.

87

ADIRONDACK

Burpee Rd.

Denton Rd.

West Rd.

9

Steele Woods Rd.

Cutting Rd.

TOWN LINE

Military Rd

Roscoe Rd.

10

West Rd.

Denton's Pond

E-Town-Wadhams Rd.

8

Old Racetrack

LEWIS
ELIZABETHTOWN

← to Keene

9N

Sadie's Father's Mill

Ford

O Roscoe

Water

Cross St.

Melba Wrisley's Town Home

Brainard's Forge Rd.

Schoolhouse Hill

SADIE CANTIN'S HOME

Old Mill Art School

Cobble Hill Rd.

Site of Windsor Hotel

Schoolhouse Hill Rd.

Elizabethtown Elementary

Deer's Head Inn

9N

to Westport →

NORTHWAY

ELIZABETHTOWN

MELBA WRISLEY'S EARLY HOME

to N. Hudson

LOBDELL FARM

Lobdell Rd.

Lincoln Pond Rd.

9

87

Scale
1 mile

N

E. Sears

Contents

Sadie E. Cantin

$\mathcal{I}$ have lived 76 years of my 88 in Elizabethtown. I married a lifelong resident of Elizabethtown, George E. Cantin, and had a son, George Lobdell Cantin. I worked as a secretary to the Superintendent of Highways of Essex County for forty years. Am now retired and have enjoyed twenty-six years of retirement and expect to continue for some time to come.

Alva M. Lewis

The Lobdell Family

$\mathcal{M}$y roots go back to 1645 when Simon Lobdell came from Hereford, England, to Milford, Connecticut. I am the eighth generation descended from this Simon Lobdell.

A fourth generation Lobdell settled in an area between Elizabethtown and Westport, evidently near Black Brook, as records show that a Capt. John Lobdell gave the property for the Black Brook cemetery.

Two brothers settled in Pleasant Valley, the area that is now called Elizabethtown. Most people knew their home as the Lobdell Farm, but it is nonexistent now. It was on the outskirts of Elizabethtown heading toward New Russia. The old Otis Mountain ski tow was located on part of that property. The Lobdell Farm is where my father, John Lobdell, was born in 1866. He had a sister and three brothers.

My mother, Lena Lewis Lobdell, was born in Jay, New York, also in 1866. Her mother died during her infancy so my mother was taken over and raised by an aunt and an uncle. She had several half sisters and brothers but was not brought up with them, so my knowledge of Mother's ancestry is limited. She knew very little about her mother. Her father, Alva M. Lewis, born in 1845, I remember as being Essex County's oldest typesetter and working for the *Elizabethtown Post.*

Mother and Dad met in Elizabethtown and were married on December 18, 1889. Keeping with the custom of large families back then, my parents raised eight children. Walter Raymond was born in 1891 and left home for Rochester to "seek a fortune." There he married Lillian Shaffer in 1920 and remained there until his death in 1931.

Anna Helen was born in 1892, married Harrison Hathaway in 1913, and was mother to six children. Anna died in 1982. Mabel Edith was born in 1894 and married Albert Wrisley in 1913. Mabel had one child and met with a horrible death at the age of thirty-two. She burned to death.

Nancy Rosamond was born in 1898. She was better known as Rosie or Rosamond. She was secretary to Judge O. Byron Brewster from the time she graduated from Albany Business College until Judge Brewster's death in 1953. Rosamond never married and died in 1975.

In 1900 Kathryn Lena, known as Kitty, was born. In 1928 she married Benjamin Rumney and they had one child. Kitty died in 1980. Next came a brother, Jerome, in 1903. "At last," Dad said, "Four girls are enough," not knowing what was coming next. Jerome married Lillian Arnold in 1926 and they had two daughters. He died in 1967. He was a typewriter expert; he sold and repaired them.

The seventh child was me, Sadie Eliza, born on May 1, 1907. I married George Edward Cantin in 1934 and we had one son, of whom I'm most proud and fond. The eighth and last child born to my parents was a boy, Theron John, in 1910. Theron was a jack-of-all-trades. He married Elsie Cutting in 1941 and had two sons. He died in 1978.

I am very proud of my heritage and grateful for being a part of these old settlers who made it possible for us to live a free and happy life over the years. Recently I was fortunate to be able to join the Daughters of the American Revolution, the DAR. A female who can prove that she had a relative who fought in the American Revolution is the only way one can join. During the process of joining I learned a lot about my ancestors.

My Childhood Home

I still remember the house of my childhood. It held mother and dad and eight children. I was the seventh, and those were the days when a child was seen but not heard.

We had a big house with six bedrooms—five upstairs and one down, a living room and dining room of normal size, a very large kitchen, a pantry, and a cellar that I still dream about.

Father was a good provider, and everything was purchased for the season, not day by day or week by week as we do now. First there was a bin that was filled with potatoes as soon as they were harvested, and a bin for apples that was filled each fall. Next there were several long shelves which held home-canned goods such as vegetables, fruits, jams, jellies, pickles, and marmalades. These jars numbered in the hundreds. Next was a stockroom which held a whole salted salmon, a whole salted codfish, several slabs of bacon, and crocks of pickles in a brine solution.

In the far back corner was a spring where Mother kept her butter and milk, being that this was the only type of refrigeration she had. This was not as inconvenient as it might sound. All Mother had to do was say, "Go get..." and there were always plenty of young legs willing to get whatever she asked for.

Father and me around 1914

Starting School

$\mathcal{A}$s the seventh child in the Lobdell family, I was another child to dress and another mouth to feed—not neglected, just taken for granted. I never went anyplace but around the neighborhood to play with other children, or to the Lobdell farm where my dad was born, and that was but a few miles away.

My brother and sisters made school sound so interesting and glorified that I was eager to attend. But not until I was eight years old was I allowed to go.

The old schoolhouse had burned and the new one was not ready for occupancy, so all the classes were being held in public places, private homes, anyplace large enough to hold a class. When I started school, the first two grades were housed in the courthouse. Can you imagine the child that I have just described walking into a big, huge room with all the rows of seats and benches, all the children, and not one did I know.

I was petrified, was told to sit down, which I did, and immediately started to cry, "I want to go home!" And home I went. They had to call my sister Rosie who was in class at the Deer's Head Inn. She came over and walked me home.

I got talked into trying it again the next day, but that also ended in disaster. I got so upset I wet my pants, and again Rosie had to take me home. Needless to say, my mother had had her fill of this nonsense and it was either or else. From then on I toughed it out, soon making friends that I still have today.

Having classes in the courthouse was very inconvenient, but the schoolhouse (the Adirondack Center Museum today) was soon finished and we moved into it. It was a real nice experience to go from the courthouse to the new school. Everything was new, clean, lots of light. Seats were very comfortable and the blackboard on two sides of the room made it easy to see the writing on it.

There were two grades in a room on the first floor; the second floor housed the four years of high school, the library, and the principal's office. In the basement was the gym where we had games and different events.

There was no lunch program then; everyone living any distance from the school had to carry their lunch. A thermos and a lunch box were not luxuries that we could afford, so our lunch box was a paper sack. It held one or two sandwiches and a couple of cookies. Only during their growing season did we have fruit, and that was only apples, pears, or grapes. If we needed something to wash the food down, we had to go into the hall and get a drink of water from the water fountain. We ate at our desks, then took off and spent time outside on the playground or walking along the street.

The new schoolhouse was greatly appreciated, not only by the students but by the residents. It was so very modern and an improvement to the village. There was no school bell because there was no tower for a bell. All the old schoolhouses had a bell in a tower and when they wanted to sound the bell, someone had to pull a rope. Not so in our modern school house. On the wall outside the building was placed an electric bell, a large metal disk shaped like an inverted soup plate. Inside, a wire rod with a round metal ball called a hammer hit the metal bell when a button was pressed indoors and made it sound.

Another improvement on the new schoolhouse was making entrances separate for "girls" and "boys," and one for the faculty. We had been used to boys crashing and crowding to get through the door first, not caring what happened to the girls who might be ready to enter the same door. Many a girl had a scraped knee or a sore butt from such rudeness. The new school provided an entrance on the east side for the boys and on the west side for the girls. Lord forbid anyone trespass!

All in all it turned out to be a very enjoyable year for me as far as first grade was concerned. Then an ill-fated fire at Dad's mill changed our lives. We moved to Westport, so I had to leave a happy class and a nice new schoolhouse.

Monday, Wash Day

*E*very Monday was a special day—summer, spring, winter, or fall. We were all up early, and had the breakfast which our mother and older sisters had prepared. For the children it was hot oatmeal, toast, and milk. We were not allowed to drink coffee until we were in our teens as mother said it "stunted our growth." I'm sure she meant to turn us against it, not really believing that it did.

After breakfast two of the older girls went upstairs armed with a pail of water and a slop jar. There were four bedrooms, each with a double bed, under which there was a vessel. This was for use in case one was "caught short" at night. Their job was to empty the vessel, rinse it out with the water they had carried up, and replace the vessel under the bed for reuse.

Each bed had to be stripped and tickings fluffed up. Why fluffed? We did not have nice, firm mattresses then, we had feathers or straw ticks. During the night while being laid on they would mat down, so each morning they were fluffed up as the bed was made.

The lower sheet was taken off the bed and the top sheet put back on for the bottom sheet. The pillow cases were changed and all was ready to be washed. Of course Mother took care of her own bed which was in a downstairs bedroom. Everybody had a bath Saturday night so all clothing was ready for the washing, too. Now for the wash day. Before leaving for work, Dad would haul in the washing machine. It was a luxury. It was set up by the sink and a hose was attached to the faucet allowing the water to run to the machine through some mechanism that turned the center agitator inside. There had to be another hose letting the water out into the sink, but that was beyond my comprehension. I was so interested in just watching the washer work.

There was a hand-cranked wringer that could be swung around so that you could wring out the clothes from the washer to a rinse, and from a rinse into a basket.

A woman came to do the laundry. She was a very large, buxom woman and as I remember had a very loud voice. I was petrified of her, as she threatened to put me in the washer if I came near her and the machine.

Early in the morning Dad had to fill a great big copper kettle with water and of course build a big fire in the stove to heat the water. The reservoir on the stove that held water had to be full and hot.

When the wash lady came, she put all the very dirty clothes in the copper pot and boiled them, while she filled the washing machine with water from the reservoir. The soap she used was some Mother had made. Some of the ingredients were lye and wood ashes. What else I don't know, but I do know it could almost eat your hands off.

The soap was shaved and put into the water so you did not have to touch it too much. The first washing was all white sheets, pillow cases, underwear, and so on. They were wrung out into a tub of cold water, rinsed, and then wrung out into a clothes basket. In the same hot water went the colored cottons, percales, etc. When all these were washed and rinsed and put through the wringer, they were ready to hang out.

Then out came the articles from the copper pot on the stove, which were the last to be washed. The wash lady never changed the water, but did add soap at times. There was also a blue rinse to put white articles through to make them look whiter. I guess some people still use it.

The wringer used to intrigue me. It was operated by hand and you had to be so careful not to get too much in it at a time or it was "sprung," which meant it fell apart and you had to stop all procedures to put it back together.

Twelve months of the year the clothes were hung outdoors to dry. We were fortunate to have a large porch that was strung up with clothesline to accommodate our wash, but it still was very difficult to hang up all those wet clothes on the cold days of winter.

My Father, a Lumberman

When I was a child, there were no buses, and a very few cars, so everyone walked to school. If in the winter we had a bad snowstorm, Father would have the horses harnessed up to the big log sleigh and take all of us to school, picking up everyone on the way. No roads were plowed or sanded in those days, so the horses had to do all the plowing as they pulled the sleigh of children. This was a big deal to us children, but I'm sure the horses did not enjoy it too much.

My father was a lumberman and a contractor. He had a lumber camp in the woods where they cut and skidded trees. After they chopped a tree down and trimmed the limbs from it, the horses would skid it to the river bank. The men lived in the camp during the winter—not an easy life as I remember hearing. The camp was crudely made, only kerosene lamps for light and no radio or TV. The food was beans and johnny cake, which soon became unbearable, and life itself was very lonesome. It was a form of hibernation.

In the spring the logs that had been skidded to the edge of the river were rolled into the river and floated down to the mill dam. To keep the logs floating and straight kept several men busy. If a log became lodged or got crosswise, they would have to walk out on the logs with a peavey to straighten the log, which often meant that they fell in the cold, icy water. A peavey was a long stick with a hinged hook at the end which helped to manage the course of a log.

The logs finally arrived at the dam and were rolled down a chute to the mill, which was just below the dam. My father's dam was just above Rice's Falls, where Lord Road meets Route 9N in Elizabethtown; part of it is still standing. This dam furnished the power for the machinery that ran in the mill. If you were to go to Rice's Falls swimming hole just below where the mill was, you could still find some of the big pipe that carried the water to the mills.

I say mills because the first mill burned October 2, 1914, and Father built the second one below Rice's Falls; it also burned two years later. As for the two mills that burned, it is of interest to note the firefighting equipment that was used in those days. There was but a wagon equipped with hose. Whenever there was a fire, men were called, and they gathered and pulled the hose wagon to the site of the fire. Needless to say, a fire a mile away was pretty well at its peak by the time help could get there.

To go back to the logs, when they finally arrived at the mill they were piled and selected. They were put through a saw that took off the bark and squared them on each side. They were then sawed up into boards of different widths and thicknesses and put into a drying kiln. In some manner there was heat forced into a room for drying lumber but I never knew how. This was the lumber Father used for building houses and other structures and which he also sold.

Logging camp

Local logging crew, circa 1908

The Good Old Days

$\mathcal{I}$often think, why do I say "the good old days" when referring to the days of my youth when there was no electricity in the house, which meant no electric refrigerator, no electric stove, no radio or TV, nothing operated by electricity. A newspaper was printed only once a week.

There were three stores in town—a drugstore which dispensed medicines and toiletries, a furniture store which sold furniture only, and a grocery store selling only canned and boxed goods during the winter, but in summer they did have some fresh fruits and vegetables. The word "shopping" was very little used. Families could travel to other towns only if they could afford a horse or two and proper wagons or sleighs.

Yet with the limited necessities, we were happy and lived a normal life. Why? Because there was no need for all the modern inventions and we experienced togetherness. During those times, families were large and they grew up as a family. They worked together, laughed together, and cried together.

At my house the day started by everyone appearing at the breakfast table at the same time. We all ate the same thing: oatmeal and toast or eggs and toast. Sometimes Cream of Wheat was substituted for the oatmeal. Each one of us had his or her duty after breakfast, such as washing and drying dishes and making lunches. Then it was off to school.

We were back home in time to help prepare supper and we all had our jobs—peeling potatoes, preparing different foods, setting the table, and anything else that Mother had not had time to do.

At 6 o'clock all was ready and we were expected to be there ready for dinner. Nobody started to eat until all were seated and grace had been said, then we could have all the food we wanted. But we were expected to eat all that we had dished out onto our plates. All plates had to be empty before dessert was served. Pie or cake was usually served and you can believe that seldom did anyone leave anything on their dessert plates.

No one was allowed to leave the table before everyone was finished unless there was a good reason and Mother allowed it, and you did need to excuse yourself when leaving. Table manners were always practiced. I guess Mother had to have some kind of order with so many children to discipline.

After dinner the kitchen work was done up, then we were allowed to play or study until 8 o'clock, which was bedtime for the younger ones; 9 o'clock was set for the older ones.

It is this togetherness that comes to mind when one speaks about "the good old days." Working together to keep warm, to keep food on the table, to find entertainment, to encourage a disciplined life, to learn and keep faith, and to laugh.

Another togetherness event that I still remember was Sunday evening. After we had spent the day sliding, skating, snowshoeing, or maybe having a good snowball fight, we would snuggle in our warm living room and Mother would sit at the pump organ to play songs for us to sing. This was a songfest I'll never forget. We would have solos, duets, and of course all kinds of voices—soprano, alto, whatever—and I'm sure we all enjoyed it as we were part of it. Pity anyone listening from the outside! Maybe a few chickadees in the trees by the bay window who nested there during the winter.

A candy pull or a fudge-making party was also a big event and a good reason to get together. All participated in the preparation, playing games while waiting for the candy to set or cool before the pleasure of eating it. Sugar, fats, and calories were of no concern in those days. If you had diabetes you did not know it and you needed the fat in food to keep you warm in winter. "Calories" was a word you had to look up in the dictionary when you needed to use it, which was seldom.

I guess that's another reason we call them "the good old days." You ate anything you wanted, any amount you wanted, and anytime you wanted it. There was no one to say, "Watch your diet!"

The Iceman Cometh

$\mathcal{M}$r. Robert Denton, a lifelong resident of Elizabethtown, owned a pond located on the back road to Lewis just outside the village. The dam for "Denton Pond" was located across the road from where Melba Wrisley and her son now live, on Cross Street above the intersection with Roscoe Road.

In the winter Mr. Denton would cut the ice into blocks and store them in a building near the pond. He would put in a large cake of ice and then a layer of sawdust, which kept the cakes from melting and from freezing together. In the summer he would deliver these cakes of ice for people to use in their "iceboxes" to keep food cool.

The icebox in those days was made from wood and lined with a metal sheeting. It had two compartments. The top was to hold a cake of ice and the bottom was for the food. You had to make sure that there was ice in the top at all times. The iceboxes came in all sizes—some had one or two shelves—but the main objective was to keep the milk, butter, and leftovers cold so they wouldn't spoil.

The one big problem with the icebox was that what went in as ice must come out as water. As the ice melted, it drained and ran down into a catch basin or pan. This had to be emptied once a day at least and you soon learned that it HAD TO BE DONE after forgetting it a couple of times. To come down to the kitchen in the morning to get breakfast prepared and find your kitchen floor flooded could sure shake you up. I know.

In 1940 when we found out that our son, George L., was on his way, we bought a Frigidaire electric refrigerator. The change was so great. We did not think we would ever use all the shelf space, but today we cannot find enough space in even much larger models.

Christmas Celebrations

*A*ll Christmases during my growing-up years are memorable to me. Not until a week before Christmas did anyone say "Christmas" or think "Christmas." Then we started to prepare food, such as fruitcakes, plum puddings, and so on. During the evenings we would pop corn and string it with cranberries to make a garland to decorate the Christmas tree. Also during that week we would cut strips of red and green paper to make a chain for decorations on the tree. Once in a while someone would get an idea for an ornament and we would make it for the tree.

This was big excitement for me and my two brothers. My two older sisters engineered the projects. The day before Christmas Father would take us out to find a tree. We would cut it down and come home bearing our Christmas tree. This surely built up our enthusiasm and the Christmas celebration was now in full swing. Dad built a tree standard and got the tree ready for us to trim. This was a full day's job. We had lots of trimmings that we had brought down from the attic, all the strings of popcorn and cranberries, and the paper chains. We were allowed to put candles on the tree but NEVER allowed to light them.

Finally it was Christmas Eve! We closed the living room door, played in the kitchen, and tried to keep quiet so we could hear Santa, but always when we got the least bit noisy Mother would say, "Did you hear him? He just left!" Off to bed we would go, dejected. We had missed Santa again this year.

In the morning our stockings that we had hung at the foot of our beds were full. We all gathered downstairs in the living room where it was warm and examined the contents of our stockings. As always, we would find a box of candy, a doll or truck, and the biggest treat—an orange. We were then allowed to open the gifts we found under the tree.

The Christmas that stands out most in my memory is the one when I was the recipient of a handmade doll. She was a white doll until you flipped her skirt over her head; she was then a colored doll. My father had made me a cradle for my doll and my sisters had made a blanket to cover her up. That was about the nicest present a girl could hope to get. My father had also made a sled for each of my brothers.

At that time the most valuable presents we got were not really appreciated—a knitted scarf or a pair of mittens that Grandmother Lobdell had made for each of her grandchildren. There were ten grandchildren in Dad's family and also four in her daughter's family. She must have stayed up nights knitting. How I would love a pair of Grandma's mittens today!

World War I

$\mathscr{I}$m really stretching my memory when I think about World War I. I remember combing the streets, or any area for that matter, for tinfoil, regardless of size. Back then gum and cigarettes were wrapped in tinfoil. We would gather it "for the cause." Nowadays we call it recycling.

I had no one from my family in the service. My father had too many children and was too old, and my one brother old enough to serve had had the misfortune of cutting off a thumb and finger in my father's shop, so he worked in a defense plant.

There was a lot of concern around our house, fear of war, which we knew nothing about—only what we heard people talk about. We had no radio, no TV, and very few newspapers.

We would attend some of the rallies they had. I remember one especially. A large bonfire was built in the middle of the village, a mannikin was dressed to represent the Kaiser, and they burned it while we danced and sang around the fire.

I will never forget the feeling I had when the news got through to us that the war had ended. A lot of celebrations and happy days ahead.

Amusements in the Teens and Twenties

$\mathcal{I}$t must be difficult for most of you to imagine how we lived and especially how we were entertained in the days I fondly remember.

Of course there was no radio, no TV, few shopping centers, nor was there the means of travel to any distant destinations. The only modern convenience we had was the telephone, if you could afford one. In those days there were three or four telephones on a line, so you heard the phone ring whenever your neighbor got a call. It gave the owner some entertainment; she could "listen in."

We did have a movie house, and it was located next to the old fire house (an office building occupies that lot today). At first it was only open Saturday nights. As time went on and business grew, it was open more often. The delight in going to the movies was not only the movie, but to get to see friends and relatives you did not see too often. It was quite a social gathering until the lights went out and everyone scampered for a seat.

They always had a comedy first and then the main feature. The evening was not complete if the film did not break at least once or twice during the show. People were content to go on with their social talks until the film was mended, and again the lights went out. Everyone got their seats and another section of the film was started. Though we had missed part of the film, no one seemed to mind. It was all part of the evening's entertainment.

There was some profanity heard in the movie hall if the film broke at the time the villain was ready to strike or the lover boy was on the verge of making love, but that too was part of the entertainment.

Another thrill we got while at the movies was when the fire siren sounded. It would lift you off your seat and of course you could hear nothing until the siren stopped.

At this time card games were very popular. People played rummy, euchre, pinochle, and bridge. There were public card games, which made entertainment for a lot of people during this period.

Dancing in those days also was very popular. A lot of square dancing was done at that time. It only took a caller and a fiddler and everyone was ready for an enjoyable evening. There were other dances, too, like the waltz, fox trot, and the two-step.

During the winter months, my sisters (who were all older than me) did a lot of entertaining by having small parties. They often invited friends in and had candy pulls. I can still see them pulling this material, which I remember as being of a taffy consistency. They greased their hands, picked up an amount of the goo, and worked it by pulling it. Then they'd place it on plates to harden.

I often call those days "the good old days" and they were just that. We knew nothing about all the modern improvements that were to come, like refrigerators, gas and electric stoves, radios, and television. So we made do with what we had. It was a happy time for all because we did not know better.

Capitol Theatre in 1936; twenty years later it was destroyed by fire

A Short Career

*A*fter twelve years of schooling and sowing my wild oats, few of which I had, I was delighted to get back to Elizabethtown where I was born. Here I had family, friends, and relatives, and found a solid ground to tread on.

For the last three years I had been in Rochester, working and going to night school. I had missed the mountains and my family, and was delighted to get word from my sister that she had found a job for me in Elizabethtown. She hardly got the words out of her mouth and I was here. I soon found my old friends who were still here and made new ones. We made our own amusements, not having too many cars or radios, and no TVs. One of our projects was putting on home talent plays, finding what talent we could among us to keep the shows going.

I had always had a big desire to sing any time that I had an invite. I found the money and time to take voice lessons from a vocal coach in Plattsburgh, a Mrs. Thomas. She was a dear little old lady; I was fortunate to have someone interested in me who could accompany me, also give me encouragement and help.

I mainly sang for our shows, solo work or in a group. I sang for some time in the church choir, soloing very often. With this and the one time that I sang at the Glens Falls Eastern Star entertainment, it just about covers my career in music.

In the early '50s I had a thyroid operation, and because of it my vocal cords were disturbed and I never was able to sing a note after that. Needless to say it was the biggest disappointment of my life. So you see, it was a short career.

Me, dressed for winter

As I Remember Elizabethtown in 1930

*I*n 1930, after twelve years away from Elizabethtown, I returned to the town that I, then and now, call home. I was delighted to get back with friends and family in familiar surroundings. I'm going back sixty-five years to tell what I remember about the village.

I'm trying to visualize how it looked to come into Elizabethtown as it was in 1930. It is difficult because only one building out of six is left. The first building in the business section was called the Cautin Block. It was a large building extending from the end of the stone wall on the Hand property—where Judge Augustus C. Hand had his offices—to the foot of School House Hill. (A gasoline service station occupies the property today.)

The Cautin Block housed several businesses. Mr. Cautin had a men's apparel store in the center of the first floor. There was an A & P on one side and on the other side William Denton operated a grocery store. Clarence Underwood had a photography shop on the second floor; he was a well-known photographer and had a large following in the area. Also on the second floor, Rita Denton had an apartment and a beauty parlor, and George W. Cantin (who was to become my father-in-law) had a barber shop and a well-furnished poolroom.

Across School House Hill (now called Court Street) was a large, three-story building owned by Charles Williams, who operated a very fine drugstore on the second floor. The building was built into the bank of the hill so the second floor was on a level with the land when you went out the back door.

Mr. Williams had a very nice soda fountain in his store, which was a big treat for the customers. He also served sodas on the porch on the north side of the building. In those days that was a big deal.

Across the street, Carl Daniels had a hardware store in what later became the Masonic Building. He and his wife and six children lived upstairs. Lawley's Restaurant was on one side of the hardware store and on the other side was a meat market operated by a Mr. Tennyson. Next door, near the river, was a granary, where they sold grain by the bagful. Farther up the river by the bridge on Water Street was Mr. Dudley's law office, built by his father who was also a lawyer.

The School House Hill was very steep and had a curve at the bottom. In the winter when the pavement was slippery, many a car ended up crashing on or against the Lawley Building. Here is a personal School House Hill experience from this time that I will share with you:

It was a beautiful, sunny, cold day and we went out skiing. On our way home I attempted to ski down this hill with its curve on the bottom. What I did not know (until it was too late) was that a horse had traveled this route minutes before and left a pile in the middle of the road at the bottom of the hill.

Not until I got to the curve did I see the "pile." You guessed it—I hit it!

Elizabethtown in the late '20s

The Elopement

During the early 1930s, politics were "hot." I mean if you were a Republican you stayed on your side of the political fence, as did the Democrats. Jobs were very scarce and you were lucky to get one. Even if you had to change your political party to get one, you did, and it was done by many. George E. Cantin was one of them. He worked for the State of New York. The Democrats were running the state at that time, and Essex County proudly stayed with the Republican Party. I worked for the County of Essex.

George E. and I both took part in hometown talent shows and we became very good friends, ending up really getting serious. Knowing what the results might be of our getting married, we held off, hoping things would change. We started planning to get married secretly, but that meant time off, getting blood tests, and a chance that the news would get out.

Then our chance came. My sister Kitty was living in Glens Falls and was a member of the Eastern Star, which was looking for a vocalist to sing at one of their entertainments and asked would I do it for them.

We decided to go to Glens Falls, I would do my act, and then we could take off, God knows where. So on a Friday afternoon we only told Mother and Dad Cantin and my sister Rosamond, and headed for Glens Falls. I do not remember a thing about the entertainment, nor singing, or what I sang. All I remember is that I told my sister Kitty I was very tired and we had a long trip home, could we be excused early and not wait for the refreshments.

She agreed, we took off, and I don't remember the roads or the towns we covered looking for a justice of the peace, but it was not until 11 p.m. that we found one in New Lebanon, New Hampshire. He was home and the house was lighted, so we stopped and explained our dilemma. He was very nice and somehow managed to get us a waiver for the blood test, married us, and his wife stood up for us. Then we were on our merry way. Yes, we found a room, stayed there that night, and returned home the next day, Saturday.

We were very careful to keep things looking as usual. I stayed home and did not move out and George stayed at his home, yet in four days the news was out.

To this day I'll never know how my mother found out that we were married, but she did and it spread in the wrong direction. The next Saturday George was fired from his state job.

In the long run it was a good thing; he went into business for himself. He studied and became a taxidermist, continuing some part of taxidermy work the rest of his life.

For an ending I want to say I did have a wedding trip. I called it one about fifteen years after we were married. We went to Canada fishing in a spot that was heavenly. We had the best kind of fishing, had all our meals served, no telephone, no radio, and at that time there was no TV. Our hosts were the most pleasant people to be with, and we had a whole week there.

A New Arrival

*A*fter six years of "wedded bliss" and beginning to think we were going to be one of the unfortunate couples that were unproductive, a phone call from Dr. Kunz announcing "Sadie is pregnant" was welcome news. I had gone to him for a rabbit test, one of the means of testing for pregnancy in those days.

We decided to keep it a secret as long as we could. This was in the early '40s, in fact it was the summer of 1940, and pregnant women were not too much in the public's eye; they stayed more in the background. Of course I had my job and wanted to keep it.

I began wearing a smock at work; smocks were being worn in offices in those days so I was able to hide my condition until August. Sometime during that month someone from one of the offices came in and said he could "spot a pregnant woman under any tent" and made me "'fess up." It was not long before my condition was town news; it sure traveled.

I had no trouble until the month of November. I became very large and clumsy, fell down four stairs, got a horrible case of hives from eating too much seafood, and so the doctor did not want me to go to the office. The result was that my work was brought to me at the house until the baby came—January 6th.

I wanted to stay home to have my baby and did. I had a nurse from Crown Point come and live in for twenty-one days. The baby was very healthy and weighed ten pounds, two ounces and was twenty-two inches long—and had a voice to match. He sure could make himself heard. I'm very glad I had my baby at home.

Justice of the Peace and Trapper

*W*illiam A. Knowlton was Justice of the Peace for a long time. He was a very big man, very tall. He handled minor crimes. If you were driving too fast, the troopers picked you up and brought you before him and he would fine and sentence you. He could also perform marriages.

In those days, the Justice of the Peace was a member of the town board and participated in, so to speak, the running of the town. Being Justice of the Peace was side work. Mr. Knowlton also had a meat market, and the other thing that I knew him to do was to trap and raise foxes.

When I was married in 1934 and moved to Water Street, Mr. Knowlton lived two doors away. He bought land along the river behind our houses. That's where he raised foxes. The cages were made of very strong fencing on all six sides; the bottom was buried in the ground.

He had the cages in a row and inside the cages he had huts that he had built. There were two foxes in a cage, male and female. They were silver foxes, black with a silver tip on the end of each hair.

These foxes were fed once a day as I remember, but what their food was I do not recall. I do know it must have included raw meat because even today you can dig up the leg bones and the skulls of large animals that were buried in that lot—most likely they are the bones of cows.

Those foxes barked, oh my goodness how they barked! But in those days things like that didn't bother us. In those days people didn't let the neighbors bother them like they do now. People would make a mention of it—"Did you hear the foxes barking?"—but no one ever complained.

The foxes were very nervous and noises bothered them. Very often one would manage to escape. Neighbors were alerted, traps were set, and a hunt was started. Usually when the fox got hungry he would go to the trap and the hunt would end.

I remember one night a large owl decided to spend the night near the fox pens and made it known he was there by tooting. This disturbed a mother of a litter of pups and to protect them she carried them from their nice warm nest to a snowbank and covered them with snow, trying to protect them. Of course they did not live through the ordeal.

Mr. Knowlton would skin the foxes and then treat the pelts and have them made into fox fur scarves. The scarf was made out of the whole thing—head, tail, and feet. There was a clip attached to the mouth that fastened to one on the tail.

You had to have a fox fur scarf if you were somebody in those days. My husband bought one for me and I think he paid $40. My husband used to go trapping with Mr. Knowlton. He loved to trap; it was a big occupation around here once upon a time.

I was thrilled when he gave me the fur scarf. I felt I really had something. It was the fad of the day. In fact, I still have it. Who knows, it may become a fad again!

Bill Knowlton (right), and his wife Florence, and furs of all kinds

The Telephone

A telephone was a luxury in my early days. It was a sizable box, attached to the wall so high one had to stand up all the while one used it. It must have had batteries. I'm not sure what the energy for its power was, but I remember if too many people used it at one time, it would start to lose its power and the reception would be very poor.

A receiver was hung on the left of the box on a hook that extended from inside. As you lifted the receiver, the hook opened the system and then you rang the bell. It sounded at the control place, which I know nothing about, but I do know it was in its infancy and quite crude at that time.

There was a mouthpiece which could be raised or lowered a distance of about six inches and a crank that you used to ring "central." Central was one person who knew everyone who had a phone and all you had to do was to ask for the person you wanted to talk to. At first there were no numbers. They had party lines, which meant several people were on that one line, and if someone was using it, you had to wait your turn.

The telephone was as good as a newspaper. When it rang, regardless for who, if you were inclined you could take down the receiver and listen in case there was news to be told. This was called "rubbering in" and it did not take long for news to spread through a neighborhood.

Spooking in the Old Days

*H*alloween was an evening of fun for all in my days of growing up. We dressed up in old clothes—the older and more hideous the better—and had parties, played games, danced, then went home with the goblins. We never thought to annoy the older people or damage property, nor did we even ring doorbells and yell, "Trick or Treat!"

One year, 1947, my friend Ruth Rafford and I decided to spook the patients in the hospital. George E. had a cousin named Ethel Trudeau in the local hospital with terminal cancer, and we knew she would enjoy it. We dressed up like two old cronies, using lots of Mother Cantin's old clothes that she had forgotten to throw away, a couple of wigs we found in the attic, lots of makeup, and lots of costume jewelry.

The hospital in those days was in the building now called Hubbard Hall. We drove right up to the hospital. We were afraid to be seen on the streets at that time of night; looking as we did we were sure to get in trouble. We went directly into Ethel's room. We spooked her and told her she was going to be carried away by some ghosts walking outside. She was thrilled with our antics, yet she had no idea who we were.

We visited all the other patients. One little old lady yelled and threw a blanket over her head and would not look at us. I think that she had been alerted and was going along with our game.

The nurses thanked us for calling and asked us to come again, so I guess all was appreciated.

Taxidermy

Taxidermy has come a long way since my husband was a taxidermist, during the 1930s, '40s, and '50s. In fact, it is quite an art in itself, learning to know how different animals live and react to surprises, how they are put together, so to speak.

A taxidermist during his first years had to be a carpenter also. He made forms for an animal out of two-by-fours and filled them with excelsior, then covered them with plaster of Paris.

Then his ability to carve came into use. He had to carve the form so as to fit the skin (the cape, as it was usually called) over it. It was a very difficult job and you did have to know quite a bit about sculpting to get the nose and eyes perfectly placed so the mount would look natural when finished.

Later on in the 1940s a new system was used for making the forms. Molds were cast from mannikins that had been molded. Then by using resin paper and a certain kind of glue, he made paper forms. These could be made ahead of time and stored for future use. They came in all sizes and many positions.

Mounting deer took up about ninety percent of a taxidermist's work. Some sportsmen would go hunting moose or elk and bring back a trophy to be mounted. Small game was not too popular for mounting. In the summer, fish would keep a taxidermist busy, but little else was mounted at that time of year.

I mentioned that taxidermy has come a long way. Instead of all the preparation of making the forms for all the animals brought in to be mounted, all a taxidermist has to do today is make a list of the different sizes of forms for the different animals he needs to mount, call his form maker, and place an order. You can mount three or four heads in a day; that would have taken you a week to do in the earlier days.

I guess you can call it progress. I just wish the profession had progressed earlier!

A Case of Mistaken Cat

$\mathcal{I}$n the fall when it was time for men to get their hunting licenses, they would congregate in the evening at my husband George E.'s shop, and swap stories. Sometimes quite a few would be present. This Halloween night was one of them. My husband was Town Clerk and issued the licenses. He took his books out to the shop where they would be handy day or night.

Ruth Rafford and Betty Prime were visiting me and we decided to spook the men. As a taxidermist, George E. was very reluctant to mount anyone's pet, especially cats. People are used to certain expressions on their pets and seldom is it captured when they are mounted, so they are not pleased with the job.

We decided to call George E. in his shop. We had a telephone in the house and in the shop, and it was normal for the shop to answer if there was one ring. We had the operator ring our number once, and of course George answered in the shop. Pretending to be women from Keene Valley, we told him we had a pet cat that had just died and we wanted it mounted. We muffled our voices and between that and our laughing, it came across to him as crying. I would not take "no" for an answer. I told him I would pay whatever he would charge, and he finally agreed and gave in. He came into the house to tell us about the "crazy" woman from Keene Valley who was going to pay big money to have her cat mounted, then went back to the shop to warn the men who were gathered that a woman was coming in, probably hysterical, and to watch their manners.

We decided to dress Ruth Rafford up and send her into the shop with our pet cat. At the time we had a beautiful orange-colored angora cat that was the pride of the neighborhood. We had to really dress up Ruth so she wouldn't be recognized. I remember she had on a bright red heavy knit sweater and we had to layer the front of it with many strings of beads to cover it. A big hat with plenty of feathers, gloves, and very outlandish clothes did it. We put the angora cat in a covered basket and sent her out the front door. Keeping her head down and a handkerchief to her nose to muffle the laughter she could not help, Ruth made her way to the shop.

By now, I had gone out to the shop one of the times when George had come in to tell about this woman (she'd called several times), and told all the men what we were up to and not to give us away. Once George came in to ask Ruth if she would help him with the base for the mount, since he had nothing prepared, and she had already started to dress up. She had to quickly get back to normal and talk with him. Still he didn't catch on.

Ruth waited the time we thought it would take someone to drive from Keene Valley and then entered the shop. She presented the basket to George on the counter, he opened it, and you can imagine his surprise when his pet cat jumped out, looked around, and disgustedly walked out on the gathering.

After Retirement

After forty years as a secretary in the Essex County highway office, I retired. Now I'm in my twenty-sixth year of my retirement and still enjoying every minute of it.

After spending eighty-five of my eighty-eight years in the Adirondacks, I can honestly say I truly enjoy life here and would not look for a better place to live. My husband, George E., and I were always avid fishing people, and we fished most ponds and rivers in the surrounding area. We always maintained a camp either on a pond or a river which we enjoyed most weekends from early spring to late fall.

In early spring, if the snow did not melt fast enough, we would take snow shoes and pack our young son, George L., in a pack basket, then take off for camp. We were always so eager to get back into camp life.

My life has not been too eventful since having retired, but I've kept very busy and very happy doing the things that I've wanted to do. At first, I did help a few old people carry on so they could stay in their homes. This is a responsibility I took on most of my adult life. For this I have been well rewarded in my old age.

In September 1984 our son George helped George E. and me celebrate our fiftieth wedding anniversary, entertaining over 100 friends, neighbors, and relatives with an open house. We had a marvelous time.

Just three months later my husband, George E., died with a massive heart attack. This of course changed my life. It happened so suddenly, I was numb for weeks, but found that I had to go on and make a new life for myself.

Turning to craft work, I learned to crochet, knit, tat, and do needlepoint. I have endless projects planned ahead. In the spring I cannot resist getting into the garden and working. We have a large vegetable garden that abounds with goodies all summer and fall. The flower gardens and beds are also a joy to work in, producing varieties of flowers too numerous to list.

I also play bridge three or four times a week and enjoy meeting with friends and entertaining at bridge parties. This pastime helps to keep me active mentally, and to keep my brain from shrinking so fast!

I now have a new interest that has come to me quite late in life. This past year I was presented with a nine-room Victorian dollhouse. It is even wired for lights. It has a fireplace on each floor and stairs leading to all three stories. Now all I have to do is paint, paper, make curtains, and furnish the house. I don't think I'll ever be bored with this life.

My advice to you is the following:

> *If you like to*
>
> > *Read a little,*
> > *View TV a little,*
> > *Visit friends a little,*
> > *And socialize a little—*
>
> *If you have*
>
> > *Projects of interest,*
> > *A skill or two,*
> > *And the ability to SMILE—*
>
> *Go ahead*
>
> > *RETIRE, you surely won't be bored*
> > *Life now becomes one BIG reward!*

*M*y name is Melba Phinney Wrisley. I was born in Wadhams, New York, on May 8, 1918. When I was five years old I moved the few miles to Elizabethtown and have lived here ever since. My father was caretaker for Mr. Ed Lee Campe's summer home for six years. I have one sister and two brothers.

I taught in the local school for twenty-eight years. My husband of forty-two years, Elverton Wrisley, passed away five years ago. I have one son, Calvin.

Our pony cart

Dressed up on my first birthday

The Four Phinney Children

*Th*ere were four of us, two girls and two boys. The girls came first, Melba and Ruth, and then two boys, Clayton and Logan, Jr. I was named for Dame Nellie Melba, the soprano, who was at the height of her singing career when I was born; Ruth was named for a hired girl we had at that time; Clayton Scott was named for both grandfathers; and Logan was named after our father. We were all blond except Ruth who had beautiful auburn hair; it always stayed in place and she could do anything with it.

Our biggest surprise one day was when our father brought home a Shetland pony and a basket cart for us. The pony's name was Prince and he became a great friend to us, especially Clayton and myself. Ruth was afraid of him and Logan was just a baby.

The basket cart had a seat on each side and would easily carry three children on a side. There was a little door at the back for us to enter. A Shetland pony is small but it's said that it is as strong as a big horse. Since this was the only pony and cart in the town, we could always find plenty of takers for rides.

Prince gave us many miles of rides. Once in a while he would run away and even tip the cart over. When this happened he stopped right away, waited for us to tip it right side up, and then went merrily on his way as if nothing had happened. We were never hurt.

When I was older I even drove him the seven or eight miles to Wadhams a few times, once to stay with cousins overnight. There was a horse stall in their garage so Prince was okay. Another time two girlfriends and I went to a friend's house to stay all night. That was on a farm so there was plenty of hay.

One winter day Clayton rigged up some harness and the first thing we knew he was "skijoring" behind Prince. Later this sport came into use in Lake Placid but I know Clayton thought of it first.

Later on we had another Shetland by the name of Tony but he never was hitched to the cart; he was more of a saddle pony.

Red Stockings

*W*hen I was about eight years old, we had my father's boss, Mr. Ed Lee Campe, for dinner. Mr. Campe was a very wealthy man whose business was manufacturing underwear and towels in New York City. My father was caretaker for his summer home here in the Adirondacks. Mr. Campe was up from the city checking on his property, so my mother went all out to serve a nice dinner.

Before the meal he called me over to him and asked what I wanted for Christmas as they always sent many gifts for us children. Without a moment's hesitation, I said, "A pair of red stockings," never even having seen any.

Well, Christmas came and also two dozen pairs of fire-engine red stockings—a dozen each for my sister and me. How we hated them! But our mother made us wear them as I had asked for them. It seemed that they would never wear out; they were really made to last. We would try to pull our skirts down to hide them but that didn't work.

Today, I think children would wear those red stockings without a thought, but in those days we wore mainly brown or black, nothing so bright.

The moral of this little story is: Don't ask for something you don't need or don't know what it is.

Dr. Gersen

$\mathcal{D}$r. and Mrs. Alexander Gersen came to the North Country in 1920 from New York City. They first settled in Westport but a few months later moved four miles west to Elizabethtown, where they bought the home on River Street that they lived in until the doctor died in 1967. Mrs. Gersen stayed a while longer in the big house but then moved back to New York to be nearer her three children.

Dr Gersen was a short, dark-haired man with a little moustache. He was always well-dressed, had a brisk, businesslike walk, and spoke with a Russian accent. My family's first experience with Dr. Gersen was in March of 1923. We lived on a farm between Elizabethtown and Wadhams. My mother was taken sick with double pneumonia and the doctor was called. Dr. Gersen drove a horse and buggy and made house calls all over Westport, Lewis, Willsboro, Essex, Keene, and Wadhams.

My mother was very sick but he pulled her through without the help of penicillin or the use of a hospital. So from then on he was our family doctor as long as he lived. As you can imagine, with four children there were many times that he was called and many office visits. No matter how sick we were, someone always tried to straighten up the house before the doctor came.

Dr. Gersen advised my father to move to Elizabethtown from the farm in Wadhams because he thought it would be better for my mother's health. He even managed to get my father work as the caretaker for Mr. Ed Lee Campe's farm and summer home. We moved and had six happy years there.

My youngest brother was born during this time and Dr. Gersen was the doctor. Years later when my son, Calvin, was born he was also the doctor. When Calvin was about two years old, he didn't talk enough to suit me. When I asked Dr. Gersen about it, he said, "Don't worry, he'll talk enough." He said his eight-year-old grandson was visiting him and he never stopped talking.

Once Dr. Gersen was asked by a local newspaper reporter if he remembered his first case. He answered, "No, but I set bones, sewed up cuts, swabbed out sore throats, treated pneumonia, hemorrhoids, sprained backs, and heart attacks. And, of course, I delivered babies—thousands of them, it seemed. Sometimes in farmhouses on the kitchen table by the light of kerosene lamps or even candles. And the 'nurse' was usually a grandmother or a neighbor."

At the time he came to Elizabethtown there was a very poor septic system and most of the raw sewage went right into the rivers. Dr. Gersen worked long and hard on the Board of Health to correct this problem. He was able to say years later that the Bouquet River that flowed through Elizabethtown was as clean and sanitary as it could be.

He realized that Elizabethtown needed a small hospital desperately, so he urged a few local people to work for one. Along with some wealthy summer people such as the Campes, the Leipzigs, the Wayman Adamses, the Boissevains, and many others, a hospital was established and called the Community House. It opened in about 1926 or 1927.

Many babies were born there and operations such as tonsillectomies and appendectomies were performed there. Two doctors from Plattsburgh did the operations—Dr. Barton, Sr., and his son. They brought necessary instruments, linens, and a trained nurse or two with them.

Many ways of raising money to start the hospital and to keep it going were thought of. Large donations were solicited, raffles were held, as well as food sales and other activities. One of the most fun were the carnivals held for several summers. The summer people engineered these. There was Mr. Leipzig, a magician, who entertained, and Mr. Gregor Piatigorsky, a world-famous cellist, who put on concerts. Our own Mrs. Musa Wakefield told fortunes in a delightful way. Also Mr. Otto Kruger, an actor from Hollywood, who had a summer home here, performed. The actress Miss Pauline Lord also summered here and helped raise money. There were booths of chance in every description.

Mrs. Gersen was a lovely lady who was a dentist and had her office in their home, too. She was interested in bringing more culture to our community and doing good works with the women. She belonged to the Women's Club, the Garden Club, and the Pottery Club. In later years she became very interested in painting. Since she lived next door to the Wayman Adams Art Studio she became acquainted with him and began taking lessons. She did many paintings, mostly of flowers and shells. They were very colorful as she had her own style.

After more than thirty-five years in our old Community House, it was felt that the hospital was too small and inconvenient and we had to have a new and larger one. Much planning went into it and more money was solicited. Today, forty years after the first one opened, we have a very fine hospital with a large staff and many specialists from Plattsburgh coming to it on certain days to accommodate the patients.

Dr. Gersen was the first Chief of Staff of the Elizabethtown Community Hospital, a position he held from 1929 to 1965. He was the Health Officer for over twenty-five years as well as being the official physician to the Essex County jail.

I'm happy to say Dr. Gersen was present for the dedication of the new hospital on September 10, 1967. He was truly dedicated to his patients. As sick as he was on the day he had to enter the hospital in Burlington, Vermont, he saw patients before he went. He died just thirteen days after the dedication, but he had seen his dream come true. He did so much for the town and the people who lived here and in surrounding areas.

After the doctor died in 1967, my family didn't have a need for a doctor until 1980, when I had to try a new one.

Our Family Home

My family moved to the house on the corner of Water Street and Cross Street when I was ten years old. I lived there for eighteen years. It was a good big house, painted white with green trim. An apartment upstairs, consisting of a kitchen, living room, bedroom, bath, and an upstairs shed, was already rented by an elderly couple who were not used to children. There were four of us noisy children but they were so good to us and never once complained of the noise. Over the years there were several other renters.

My sister and I had a large bedroom upstairs. Downstairs there were a living room, dining room, kitchen, two bedrooms, and a bathroom. Also a nice little pantry, and an enclosed shed where we kept the coal.

We had a nice lawn all the way around the house since we were on a corner lot. My father always had a good garden. But he found it hard to work in it as every time he went out, several men would stop to visit. He was a great visitor and really enjoyed the talks.

My mother was a very good cook and even though money was scarce she always set a good table. But one brother had to have peanut butter at every meal; he preferred it to all other food. It was bought in a three-pound pail. Groceries were bought just once a week, on Saturday. Milk was delivered to the door by a milkman.

We had some friends who would stop on summer evenings. They had five children and we would have a great time playing Red Light, Hide and Seek, and Hop Scotch. The bugs and mosquitoes didn't seem to bother us nearly as much as they do now!

My First Days at School

$\mathcal{I}$t doesn't seem possible but it was more than seventy years ago that I entered first grade with high hopes of adventure. The school I attended is the building at the top of School House Hill in Elizabethtown that has since been turned into the Adirondack Center Museum.

My first and second grade teacher was Miss Lucy Cutting, a very dear lady. Both grades were in the same room. After you passed first, you just moved to the other side of the room. One thing I remember Miss Cutting wearing on my first day was a long string of beads which came below her waist. I had never seen anything like that before.

Our first reading book was *The Winston Reader*, copyrighted in 1920. This was way before the "Dick and Jane" books. The first story was "The Little Red Hen" which I loved. I would read it to my mother and father and they thought it was wonderful until they realized I had memorized the whole thing and really didn't know one word from another. I was lucky enough to find one of these readers last summer at a book sale for ten cents and would you believe, it had the name of one of the boys in my class!

On the first day of school children always came with new dresses and pants and always new shoes. My mother had worked hard to make a dress, and I also had new shoes which were supposed to last the year. But as luck would have it, it just poured as we were let out at noon to go home. We lived about a mile from school and there were no buses at that time, so my neighbor from across the road, who was in sixth grade, said we could walk to the house where her father was painting. We did so, and climbed in his truck. We weren't much better off there, as it leaked like a sieve. We had to wait quite a while for him to finish his work. My mother wasn't too pleased when she saw the condition of my clothes.

Well, I did pass first grade and was able to move to the other side of the room. The one thing that stands out was learning the multiplication tables through twelve times twelve. How we did it, I don't know, but we had to stand in front of the class and go through them all. No calculators then. But they certainly have been helpful all my life.

The children all loved Miss Cutting. In later years she only taught second grade. Strange as it may seem, when she was ready to retire, she spoke to me about applying for her job, which I did, and I remained as a teacher in the second grade for twenty years. My son was one of my pupils. Then time to retire.

Art Colony in Elizabethtown

In the summer of 1920 Mr. Wayman Adams and his wife, Margaret, were on their way from New York City to Lake Placid. They had camped along the way. He was a young artist who had been commissioned to paint a portrait of a wealthy cotton broker who was vacationing in Lake Placid. One of their last camping spots was in Scrabble Hollow on the Hurricane Mountain Road just outside of Elizabethtown.

They put up their tent on one side of the road, paying no attention to an old abandoned farmhouse on the other side. But in the morning they went over to see what was there. There was a rushing brook on one side of the house and right away they fell in love with it. By fall Mr. Adams had accumulated enough money from painting portraits to buy it. As time went on they made a large studio out of an old barn and did extensive work on the house.

The people of Elizabethtown did not realize that they had a famous painter in their midst. But after a few years the Adamses's son's tutor begged for lessons and some people from the village wanted lessons so soon six or seven students were painting in the studio.

About this time Wayman Adams came up with the idea of buying an old grist mill in the village and it was turned into the Old Mill Art School. That was in 1933 and soon it attracted very fine teachers and students from all over. Many of them became famous. There were bedrooms for them at the Mill and also a dining room for meals.

It was a common sight on almost any day to see several artists painting around the village. At first we may have made fun of them, but we soon realized we were very lucky to have such talent in our town. On certain days it was possible for anyone to go to the Mill and observe Mr. Adams doing a portrait. He used many local people as subjects.

Ever since those days many local people have taken up painting and have turned out many lovely pictures. More than one exhibition has been held.

Wayman Adams paints Gregor Piatigorsky

Louis Untermeyer

$\mathscr{I}$n 1928 Louis Untermeyer, the noted poet and anthologist, bought the home owned by Mr. and Mrs. Frank Bartlett located on a back road out of Elizabethtown that leads toward Lewis in a roundabout way. Mr. George Bartlett, father of Frank, had built the house many years before, probably in the 1840s. He also had owned many acres of land in all directions from the house. A lovely brook tumbles down the hill on one side of the house and makes a pretty sound as it rushes by. Mr. George Bartlett gave the house the name "Stony Water," by which it is still known today.

Mr. Untermeyer arrived in town with his wife, Jean Starr, a poetess. He had been married to her for about twenty years, then divorced, married another poetess for two years, divorced, and remarried Jean Starr. They were re-divorced in 1933. Then he married Esther Antin in 1944 and divorced her in 1948. His last wife was Byrna Ivens, another poetess and writer, whom he married the same year. She was still with him when he died in December of 1977 at the age of ninety-two. Along this rocky road he had three sons who attended the local school.

Mr. Untermeyer asked his friend, the artist Rockwell Kent, to renovate and enlarge his home, which was too small for his family and all the people who visited. Two bedrooms were added along with more bathrooms, a porch, woodshed, and a beautiful new living room which was pine panelled, with many bookshelves and a lovely fireplace. But Mr. Kent didn't like it—said "it looked like the inside of an elegant casket." Mr. Kent tried to brighten up the room and take away the gloomy feeling by hanging one of his own flashy oil paintings above the fireplace. He gave it to the Untermeyers.

Mr. Untermeyer built a small studio up in the woods for himself where he could concentrate on his writing. It was always left open when they went away, so a few times we children would wander in, looking at pens and pencils on the desk which the famous man had used. It was exciting.

Sometime during the early 1940s my neighbor John Hooper called me to ask me to help him serve a dinner party at the Untermeyers. I said, "Sure, would be glad to." It was a great experience just to get in the house. Mrs. Liberty, a very nice lady from Scotland, cooked the meal. John and I had to set the table with beautiful china and crystal goblets. Probably ten or twelve guests were there.

I imagine many famous and notable people were present— possibly even Robert Frost, who was a close friend of Mr. Untermeyer's and made many visits there—but I was too busy to notice. They had a lovely evening with much talking, and I was happy that I didn't spill anything or make a bad mistake. We had to clean up after the meal and help with the dishes. For all my worrying and work, I do remember that I was given one dollar.

The Untermeyers left Elizabethtown in 1948 for Connecticut. The house has had several owners since then and today it is a very successful bed and breakfast. The owners have added many new features and built several other cottages. It is most attactive.

The Phinney Horsemen

My father, Logan O. Phinney, and my grandfather, Scot E. Phinney, were great lovers of horses. They lived on a farm in Brainards Forge, a small settlement near Elizabethtown, where they kept many horses at various times.

When cars were first coming into the area, my grandfather was offered a car dealership but he refused, saying it was "just a passing fancy," and he would stick with his horses. So he lost out on a good business venture.

My father was an avid participant in trotting races at county fairs during the summer. There were quite a few men who were interested in racing and kept horses right in the village. Some were Percy Egglefield, Barney Cross, Rob Dougan, Jack Lamb, Walt Johnson, Net Denton, Tommy Cassevaugh, Eldred Hutchins, and Rossie Carson.

These men made a race track just outside of the village in someone's pasture where they held races on Saturday afternoons during the summer and fall. They even built a judge's stand with a room underneath for selling soda and other refreshments. It is still standing today. They really had a good time there. In later years, when I learned to drive a car, it was up to the old race track to practice because I would be safe there, and probably other people on the road were safer, too.

One Saturday in the winter, sometime in the 1930s, the men decided to hold a race on Water Street, in the main part of town. The street was blocked off to traffic from the bridge to the top of the hill where it meets Route 9N. I have no idea who gave them permission but it was done, and the horses raced up Water Street. This was just a one-time affair. For what reason remains unknown.

Another time the men were invited to Lake Placid for a race on Mirror Lake on the ice. Quite a few men there were horsemen and enjoyed a good race. It was very cold but they made the trip, horse and all. My father made a new track record with his horse, named John Madden.

John was an ungainly looking horse, not a bit like our idea of a race horse, but how he could go! I know, for one day I teased Dad to let me drive John Madden up the back road to Lewis. Going up was fine, but after turning around for home we fairly flew back. But we made it after a few anxious moments and me losing my hat.

The horsemen had ice races on Lake Thrall in Lewis, too. It was mighty cold standing around watching the horses. The cars had poor heaters or none at all at that time, but still we enjoyed the good fun.

This pastime of racing provided many happy and busy times for my father and the other men. Now they are all gone and there is not a racehorse in town. Just an abandoned judge's stand and an overgrown race track are left.

My grandfather, Scot E. Phinney

Vergery Carson - Horsewoman

*T*here was a young lady by the name of Vergery Carson who became one of the best racehorse drivers in the North Country. She was born in Lewis to Mr. and Mrs. Rossie Carson. It might be noted that her nephew, Brian Carson, became a world-famous stunt driver, but with cars, not horses. And her brother Ross was an air force pilot, so he was in a daring profession, too.

In 1930, when Vergery was fourteen, she competed in the Westport Fair trotting races against many experienced men drivers who certainly weren't happy to have a young girl beat them. The next year she drove at the fair in Great Barrington, Massachusetts, and was rated very highly for her skill and fairness by all the famous drivers who competed against her.

One of her horses was named Sage King, and took top money for Vergery many times. In the winters of 1931 and '32, Saturday afternoon races were held on Lake Thrall in Lewis, and Sage King was always the winner in his class of trotters. On one Saturday, even though there was four inches of water on the ice, the races went on just the same to the delight of the large crowd. In spite of the hard going, Sage King won three heats.

On December 29, 1931, at 1:15 in the morning, with the thermometer registering 44 degrees below zero, a fierce fire broke out in the horse barn of Mr. Fred Fortune in Lake Placid where thirty-eight horses were stabled. There were several horses from Elizabethtown in the barn, as they had been racing there. They called the men from here to come over to help. As they were going through the Cascade Lakes between here and Lake Placid, they began to see horses running wild, since they had been turned loose. Of the thirty-eight horses in the barn, thirty-seven were saved. The one that perished belonged to Vergery. He was valued at $3,000. I think it was Sage King, who had brought her so many victories.

At the May 30, 1933, Memorial Day celebration in Saranac Lake, she was touted as a special attraction and drove in the trotting races. Women racers were unheard of at the time and she had been so successful that everyone wanted to see her race.

After such a spectacular career behind her, Vergery's life was cut short at the age of twenty when she contracted typhoid fever while racing in Vermont in 1936. She was greatly admired by the other race drivers. After all, she held track records in Vermont, Maine, and New Hampshire, as well as New York.

Circus Days in Elizabethtown

*B*ack in the 1930s when there wasn't too much excitement and it was impossible for families to travel any distance for fun, there would be one great day in town for the children and also the grownups. The circus would come to town.

It was held on the Elser Lot on Water Street right next to the present Elizabethtown post office. The circus people would arrive about 6 a.m. to put up tents and get all ready for the big show that afternoon. Many of the young boys in town would gather there by 5 in the morning to be sure to get jobs watering the animals. My two brothers were among them, since it meant a free ticket for each of them.

The elephants—probably there were two—would help put up the tents. Sometimes the handlers would take the elephants right down to the river to drink and cool off. This was very handy as the Bouquet River was right in back of the field.

Everything was set up by 10 a.m. The circus people would then take naps in their trucks or wagons until show time. There were afternoon and evening performances.

Other animals in the show included two or three tigers, monkeys, little dogs, and a few ponies. Pony rides were given in the afternoon.

There was a cooking tent connected to the circus and meals were served to the help and the performers right there. I am sure that popcorn and soda pop were sold there to the audience. One of my sources was pretty certain that depression glass dishes were sold either outright or by buying chances.

The circus gave Mr. Elser, who lived right across the street, about ten free tickets and possibly ten dollars for the use of the field. This seemed adequate at the time as they did a fine job of cleaning up after themselves and were out before daybreak the next day, and Mr. Elser said it saved him the bother of mowing the field. The owner of the circus and the managers stayed at Mrs. Elser's, as she ran a rooming house. She did not feed them, however.

A young married couple from Canada performed on the tightrope. She was a very pretty blond girl and he had dark hair. They made a striking couple. They used to practice in the back yard at Elsers' home.

Artists from the Old Mill Studio were very busy painting pictures of all the action. They set up their easels on the sidewalk across the street.

The last circus held on the Elser lot was in 1946, but later the Franzen Circus put on their show on Noble Terrace, across the street from the Elser lot. At that time there were just two houses up there—Mr. Joe Laraby's and Dr. Kunz's—so there was plenty of room.

But a terrible tragedy happened. A young lady trapeze performer fell during her act and broke her neck. She had no protective net. Her mother and father had come especially to see her perform. She was just carried out quietly and the show went on. The audience didn't realize how serious it was until much later.

The last circus of the time was held in the early 1950s. Probably one reason the circus stopped coming was that people could now go to bigger places and see bigger and better shows. Also it was too expensive for the small shows to travel to these little towns.

Heydays in Elizabethtown

$\mathcal{T}$he so-called "Heydays in Elizabethtown" extended from the 1930s into the 1950s. Many wealthy and famous people came here for the summer. Many of them had their own homes here, and brought their own household help and chauffeurs. These people were a great addition to our summers and many of them did much to keep our hospital, called the Community House, going. It was an exciting time.

Mr. and Mrs. Ed Lee Campe, owners of Ledgewood, were great believers in the need for a hospital in town and contributed thousands to it. When the hospital was closed in 1936 due to financial problems, Mr. Campe did much, even to the remodeling, to see that it reopened in 1938. Their friend Mrs. Lila Leipzig sold hundreds of raffle tickets to raise money. No one was safe from her. Her husband, Nate, was a famous magician.

It was exciting when Mr. and Mrs. Otto Kruger and daughter, Ottilie, arrived from Hollywood with several cars, maids, and chauffeur to spend the summer on Wood Hill. Also Miss Pauline Lord and Mr. Ed Flammer came from the acting world.

Mr. and Mrs. Ludwig Baumann, owners of a large furniture store in New York City, had a lovely home here. The Hulberts own it today. Mr. Louis Untermeyer, the famous poet and anthologist, also had a year-round home here.

Mr. and Mrs. Wayman Adams decided to establish an art colony in Elizabethtown and called it The Old Mill. It was very successful and many would-be artists studied there. Any day we could see artists painting local scenes. Mr. and Mrs. Thomas Lamb had a summer home on Water Street; he was a famous architect in New York City.

Then for the musical side of the picture. Mr. Gregor Piatigorsky, the world-famous cellist, and his wife bought property here. From this connection came Mr. and Mrs. Ivan

Galamian, who established Meadowmount, a world-famous music school, which is still going today. Many young people have strengthened their violin skills here.

Miss Fannie Levine and Miss Vera Giles had a camp here. Miss Levine played for church services and other occasions. Mr. and Mrs. James Rosenberg loved these mountains. Their home was on Hurricane Mountain Road. We can thank him for Cobble Hill Golf Course; he bought it and presented it to the town.

Mr. and Mrs. Sol Goldberg came from Chicago and bought property here. He had invented the hump hair pin and the famous bobby pin.

Mr. and Mrs. Ira Younker came first to the Windsor Hotel as guests, liked the town, so bought property and spent summers. Eventually they thought we should have a Colonial Garden in the back of the Adirondack Center Museum. So that was their gift to the town. We all know what a beautiful spot the garden is in the summer and how lucky we are to have it.

These were known as the good old days but I think they are pretty good right now, if we could just slow down and enjoy them more.

Windsor Hotel Days

*Y*ears ago we had two large, beautiful hotels in Elizabethtown. They were just across Route 9 from each other. One was the Windsor Hotel and the other the Deer's Head Inn. In the spring of 1937 I needed summer work as I was a student at Plattsburgh Normal School, so I applied at the Windsor for a waitressing job.

Mr. and Mrs. Parent had owned the hotel for many years and had run it very successfully. They passed away in 1936 and left it all to their niece, Mrs. Fay, who had no experience at all in running a hotel. But she came in the spring and supervised the opening and cleaning, getting ready for what she knew not.

That was my first summer of working there. Mrs. Fay was a lovely lady but it was a hard summer for her, keeping everyone happy. Some of the guests tried to put something over on her, as they would order two entrees and actually eat them. But she soon put a stop to that.

It was scary the first time I walked into that huge dining room. There was a beautiful hardwood floor which gleamed with new varnish, lovely large windows along one whole side looking out at the street, and more tables and chairs than I had ever seen. But there was a wonderful woman in charge of the dining room by the name of Mrs. Mae Pettingill who took me under her wing and taught me the correct procedure for waiting table.

My first table to wait on was filled with the hotel's six musicians. They went by the name "The Gold Coast Orchestra of Boston." They were very good musicians. They were college boys, too, and how they could eat and drink milk! I waited on them all summer.

After a few days I was given my first real customers. They were Mr. and Mrs. Gabriel who had come for the summer from New York City. Very nice people. He picked a blue bachelor's button every morning from the Windsor garden for his lapel. Then I was given a few more tables. As time went on it built up to seven tables, which was the most any waitress had.

A little different custom at the Windsor was that the diners wrote their orders on a pad and we went to the kitchen and filled them. After the meal finger bowls were passed, unheard of today. One lady cleaned her false teeth in one of them, which was the talk of the dining room workers for a while.

We had bus boys to carry the real heavy trays and also to take dirty dishes to the kitchen. We girls were responsible for washing our own goblets and silverware, changing the linens, and setting up our tables after each meal. It was bedlam trying to wash the goblets and silverware as there was just one sink and twelve or fourteen girls. But most of us were young and easy to please. We also had to polish all the silverware once a week, and be sure we had fresh flowers on our tables. We picked the flowers in the Windsor garden.

Windsor Hotel, May 16, 1936, with ice around fountain

Also, about every eight days our turn would come to sweep the whole dining room after breakfast. Two girls would work together. When we were finished with the work after a meal we would cross the road to "Blue Heaven," a rundown cottage where we lived. There were plenty of bedrooms but only one bathroom. There were always uniforms to wash by hand and then they had to be ironed, or we would just rest until the next meal.

There was no time off; we worked three meals every day for the season from July 1st until Labor Day. Many of the guests came for the entire season. The dining room could accomodate 100 guests and we did fill it two or three weekends in August but the rest of the season the count was lower.

There were three men cooks at the ranges, a little old man who did the baking and desserts, two young fellows making salads and squeezing orange juice in the morning, a steward overseeing the kitchen, and a boy running the dishwasher. It was a noisy, busy place.

Very good meals were served. For instance, on a Fourth of July menu from that time we find relishes, two juices, three soups, roast turkey or prime ribs of beef, five vegetables, three salads, and five desserts—apple pie, strawberry shortcake, lemon meringue pie, petit fours, and maple walnut sundae. Also fruit or cheese and crackers. It should have pleased everyone.

In the winter of 1938, Mrs. Fay sold the hotel to Mr. Guy Davenport. He was a fine man with hotel experience. He had run hotels in Hawaii, Canada, and other places in the United States. He brought many new ideas with him. For example, he wanted covers for the backs of the dining room chairs. My mother made them out of a floral-patterned fabric with a blue background for 100 chairs. They looked very pretty and dressed up the dining room. Mr. Davenport was a bachelor at the time and very handsome. He was very popular in the village, too.

Most of the guests were retired people who came for the summer. There were practically no young families with small children. Some of the main activities to keep them entertained were bridge and rummy, Ping-Pong, croquet, badminton, bingo at night, golf, and archery. Dancing was enjoyed in the ballroom at 8:30 p.m. on Wednesday and Saturday nights, when music was furnished by the Gold Coast Orchestra of Boston. Swimming was enjoyed by some at the Windsor pool, which was a fresh water pool in back of Judge Brewster's home a short walk away.

Mr. Davenport brought a beautiful Hawaiian young lady to sing for the guests. Her name was Momikai and she entertained with songs and dance of old and new Hawaii. She was very nice and seemed to enjoy it here in our mountains. In later years she was a featured singer at the Persian Lounge in New York City.

Once during the summer a picnic was held for the guests at Lincoln Pond, a few miles from the village. They really enjoyed it. Some of the dining room staff went along to serve the food. Also once a year they had a ride on Lake Placid in the "Doris," a very nice steamboat. A box lunch was prepared for each one who went and it was a lovely trip away from the bustle of the dining room.

From an old brochure we find that room rates were very reasonable. A single room with bath was $12, $14, or $16 and a double room with bath was $20, $24, or $28. It said there were eighty-five bathrooms in the building. The rates listed included excellent meals.

All rooms had telephones and were heated if necessary. An automatic sprinkler system for fire protection was in place. The hotel was recommended by Duncan Hines, who published a guide to hotels.

Mr. Davenport got married to a very nice woman two or three years later and she helped him in many ways at the hotel. In 1954 he sold the Windsor to Al and Annabelle Kurtz, who added a motel and a swimming pool to help draw in more guests.

But the days of the big hotels were coming to a close. They were too expensive to operate for just two months of the year.

It was decided to hold a big two-day auction at the Windsor in October 1965. Everything sold. After all the furnishings were sold, Mr. Paul Calkins, the auctioneer, called for bids on the empty hotel. There was dead silence. After two or three more calls, one voice was heard to say, "One dollar!" Mr. Calkins said, "Sold." Mr. David Cross now owned the empty building but just overnight. He could not get insurance on it so was refused ownership.

The building was torn down in 1968. It was a sad day for the village to see it go as it had been here from about 1878, when it was run by Mr. Orlando Kellogg, who was in Abraham Lincoln's cabinet. In fact, Mr. Lincoln used to say, "I would have some pretty sad days, if it weren't for Mr. Kellogg's stories."

My First School

*W*ell, it finally happened. I had my first real school, not the make-believe school I had played all those years. After graduating from Plattsburgh Normal School in 1939, I was delighted to be offered a position in the Deerhead School, a one-room District School in a settlement ten miles north of the main school in Elizabethtown. The pay was very low compared to today, but at the time I wondered what I would do with all that money—$95 a month. I soon found out.

I had only been in a one-room school once before as a guest for a day, so I really didn't know what to do or what to expect. Plattsburgh Normal had done nothing to prepare me for it. But full of enthusiasm and with shaky legs, I started out for the first day, which was September 5, 1939.

I was met at the school by ten boys and two girls, all anxious to see the new teacher. When things settled down I found we had three children in first grade, two in second, three in third, one in fourth, no fifth grade, and three in sixth. Now to figure out how to fit all the classes into each day. But these children were the best and I remember no real trouble with any of them.

We seldom saw anyone else all day. The principal came only two or three times a year and there was no nurse to call on for help. But, thank goodness, we never needed one. A bus driver with a station wagon brought the children in the morning and picked them up at night. Two of the boys walked.

The room was fairly large with a good supply of books, maps, and metal storage bookcases. No electricity and no running water. It would get pretty dark in the winter afternoons. Every morning two of the big boys would go over to the brook and get a pail of water for drinking and hand washing. There were two chemical toilets in the building. Also a large woodshed was attached. There was a big wood stove which the janitor started every winter morning, but it was up to us to keep it going during the day. Only once did it go out and that was because we were so busy and interested in getting the school decorated for our Christmas program, to which all the parents came.

One boy never did learn to spell while I was there. Every spelling word was written something like this: ukpe, dbsr, or lmpk. I have often wondered how he made out.

At the end of the first year we decided to have a picnic at Po-ko-Moonshine Mountain. So I made two trips in my car to get the children there, about ten miles one way. My sister joined us to help out, but the first thing that happened was one of the big boys found a snake just as we landed and had my sister halfway up the mountain before I could stop him. But we all had a great time, as I remember.

My high school graduation dress!
It's 1935 and I just turned 17.

The second year started out with three new boys in first grade, two in second, one in third grade, and three in fourth. We had lost our three sixth graders as they went down to the main school as seventh graders.

School started on a Tuesday, and on Thursday a little four-year-old girl appeared. She wanted to come to school too, as her brother had had so much fun the year before in first grade. As it happened, the principal chanced to visit that day so I told him and he said she couldn't stay as she was too young, which she was. But she came right up to him and said, "I can read." He said, "All right, let's hear you." So she stood up on the recitation bench and read the first story with the book upside down!

He said, "All right, you can stay." I was very pleased as she was a cute little girl. She lives in Texas now and came to see me three years ago, telling me that she has three degrees after her name. She had her son with her and he was working on his Ph.D., which he earned the following year. So I guess it all turned out fine.

During the summer after the second year the principal came to me and asked me to move to the main school and take over the fourth grade. So I did, but first I made a visit to all the families in Deerhead to say goodbye and wish them all well. That school has now been turned into a very nice home.

A New School

*W*hen I was transferred from the one-room Deerhead school in September of 1941 to the main school in Elizabethtown, my classroom turned out to be in the Lamb Home at the foot of School House Hill. There were three grades in that building; mine was fourth with fifteen children. It was a very small room, just barely enough space.

We had to walk the children up the hill to the main school for lunch, gym classes, and any programs which happened to be going on. Also for the busses at night. So you see, we were on the road quite a bit, no matter what the weather. But we never lost a child. It was good that the traffic was light.

After a year and a half we were moved to the main school where I taught for five more years with many fine students. I lived at home with my mother and father and they were busy, happy years. World War II was on and we were busy with the war effort and making do without a lot of things. Meat was scarce and sugar was rationed along with other things. My two brothers both went to service along with my future brother-in-law.

Once a week someone from the post office would come to the school to sell savings stamps. As I remember, they were ten cents a stamp and were pasted in a book, which when filled could be redeemed for an $18.75 bond.

In the fall the older boys went out to gather milkweed pods which were used in the war effort for life-saving jackets. The boys had quite a contest to see who could get the most.

After five years in this school, my principal thought it was time for me to move on to meet new people and have new experiences. He and his wife even took me to Fort Plain in central New York for an interview but I declined the offer of a position there as the school was on a hill and you had to climb 100 stairs to get to it. One of the other women being interviewed counted them. With a car it was better but I had no car.

Eventually I found an opening in Cortland in second grade and was very happy there for one year. But as they say, "Boy meets girl," and it was time to marry, so once again I came back to Elizabethtown where I have lived ever since.

World War II Memories

$\mathcal{N}$early everyone can remember exactly where they were when they heard about the attack on Pearl Harbor by the Japanese on December 7th, 1941. My mother and I were returning from a nice weekend in Albany with my sister and friends. Along the way, I happened to turn on the car radio. We were shocked and couldn't understand what had happened. The announcer was talking so fast and about such a horrible thing.

We couldn't wait to get home to hear about it from family and neighbors. But we were traveling Route 9, which took a good four hours with all its crooks and turns and small towns. No Northway at that time.

When we finally arrived home, no one knew any more than we did but we knew we were in trouble and war would be declared. The next day my brother and some other boys who were working in Connecticut at a war plant came home to have their fathers sign for them to enlist. They were too young to do it themselves. My father refused and sent my brother back to work. But later on he did enlist in the Navy and saw heavy duty in the Pacific. We had many worries about him when we didn't hear from him for weeks at a time.

My younger brother went in the Navy, too, but much later. He was at Bainbridge, Maryland. My husband-to-be was in the Army for almost five years. He was one of the very first in Essex County to be called up right after Pearl Harbor. He saw duty in Africa and Italy in the 5th Army Headquarters. We did not meet until after he was discharged. Thank goodness all three came home safe and sound.

We put a large world map on the dining room wall. A common pin was put in for each person we knew in the service showing where they were stationed. The map was quite a topic of interest when visitors came since many local boys were in the service.

Although most of the servicemen were going through many hardships, we on the home front had some, too. Meat, sugar and other things were rationed. You could only get a new pair of shoes if you had a coupon. New cars were out of the question. Also household appliances were not to be had. We had to make do with what we had.

Red ration stamps were used for meat, butter, fats, and cheese and there were blue stamps for other products. The stamps were supposed to make it equal for all and prevent the black market. To get the stamps everyone had to be registered.

In 1943 or 1944 an Army bus used to come to Elizabethtown on Monday nights to pick up any young ladies who would like to go over to the Lake Placid Club to dance with the soldiers there. The Club was used as an R&R place for men who had seen much combat. An Army band played excellent music and the bus was full each week.

Each girl dressed up for the dances. We wore the best we had. The Club at that time was in beautiful shape, and it was a treat just to be able to go there. Girls from other towns were bussed there, too, so it made quite a large crowd. I'm sure we brought some cheer and friendliness to many lonesome young men who were anxious to get home. The bus brought us back to Elizabethtown about 11 p.m.

On May 8, 1944, about 8 a.m. we turned our radio on to get war news. President Truman was talking and he announced that the war in Europe was over. It was my birthday and was one of the best birthday presents I ever had. It was called VE Day for "Victory in Europe". Now to finish the war in the Pacific. But that took over a year to accomplish.

Then, on August 15, 1945, a *New York Times* headline announced in big print: "Japan Surrenders, End of War!"

It was a great time for a celebration. Another headline said: "New York goes wild as millions throng the streets" and "World blows its top at the news."

Evening Group

Close to fifty years ago an elderly lady by the name of Mrs. Mary Bullock, better known as Mollie Bullock, returned to her hometown of Elizabethtown after working for many years in New York City. After settling in and assessing the situation she decided it was time to start a Young Ladies Group in conjunction with the Congregational Church. So she invited a few of us to her home one evening. We really didn't know why we were there, but before the evening was over we found out, and had formed a Young Ladies Group.

There was already a Women's Group in the Church but, of course, we weren't interested in that, nor did they really want us. They met in the afternoon one day a week to work on bazaar articles and plan suppers. Since most of us were working days we decided to meet one night a week. Thursday night seemed like a good choice.

We made plans to do a lot of sewing so we would have a good bit to sell at the Summer Bazaar. However, it seems that Marguerite Agnew was about the only good sewer in the crowd, so she kept the sewing machine buzzing. The only thing I was allowed to do was baste, which could be pulled out.

The group started in the fall and we kept going all through that cold winter. We never cancelled a meeting for cold weather or heavy snow. If a car got stuck, we all pushed. We met at each others' homes, carrying two suitcases filled with our work and materials. It was some job carrying those two heavy suitcases from place to place.

One very good part of the evening was the socializing that went on and the great refreshments that were served. As time went on we gathered new members until we had at least fifteen or sixteen in the group. We had such good fun those evenings we hated to leave. Sometimes it would be 11:30 before we got home.

One winter, probably in 1945, we decided to have a progressive supper. None had ever been to one but it turned out just fine. Of course, it was held in January on one of the coldest nights but it didn't bother us one bit to take off our wraps, overshoes, hats, and mittens at seven houses.

Our first stop was at Emma King's on Noble Terrace for appetizers, then on to Ruth Dudley's on Court Street for a soup course. My house on Water Street was next for fried oysters, which my parents had been busy preparing. They had never made them before and never did afterwards, but they were very good. Then up Water Street to Elsie Longware's for a salad.

We were getting filled up, but we knew we had a lot of eating yet. Now it was time to go to Elizabeth Bey's on the other side of Water Street for a chicken meal. It was delicious with peas and carrots in a beautiful divided silver dish.

Bundling up again we set out for Grace Barnett's on Water Street for the most fantastic angel pie. It was pure white with chocolate shavings on top. Our last stop was at Aletha Watson's on Maple Street where we had cheese and crackers and coffee. We really couldn't move at that point. That supper was probably one of the longest ever in Elizabethtown—it took from 6 p.m. to 12 p.m. Over the years we have had two more progressive dinners, but none as elaborate as the first one.

In later years, as we grew older, we decided the nights were not as much fun as they used to be, so we now meet on Thursdays at the Parish Hall from 10 a.m. to 2 p.m. One person is chairman for the month and furnishes dessert for lunch that month. We each bring our own sandwich. It works out very well. We have raised much money for the Church with our bazaars, dinners, lunches, flea markets, and mother-and-daughter banquets.

Some of the original members are still active. Some have moved away and others are deceased. But we are grateful to Mrs. Bullock for her initiative in getting us started.

The name has been changed from Evening Group to Women's Fellowship as has the name Congregational Church to United Church of Christ, but it's still the Stone Church at the top of School House Hill.

Flash Flood

One day in early July of 1947, my mother and I were sitting on the porch of our home at the corner of Water and Cross streets. We were busy making plans for my wedding, which was scheduled for July 19th. It had been a nice, sunny day, but we happened to notice that the sky was getting very dark up Cross Street, in the direction of Lewis. We knew it must be raining hard up that way but the sun was still shining in Elizabethtown and not a sign of rain.

Just out of sight of our house there was a very pretty pond right along the side of the road. It was the village swimming pool. It was known as Denton's Pond because a Mr. Rob Denton owned it. The boys had put a platform on a high tree by the dam and many of them used it to dive from. I never saw a girl use it. Just up the road a bit there was a fairly good beach and the water there was safe for the youngest of children. Mr. Denton cut ice on the pond in winter and stored it in an icehouse by the pond.

As my mother and I watched the sky, it got darker and darker up that way and suddenly we were amazed to see big chunks of ice and water pouring right down Cross Street. We learned later that there had been a cloudburst and the dam, being pretty old, couldn't handle that amount of water and just gave way, taking the icehouse with it. Mr. Denton nearly drowned, but he had a large, strong girl working for him and she saved him. He had grabbed a tree and was hanging on for dear life.

The water did not come clear down to Water Street, where our house was, but somehow it turned to the left and made its way to the village where quite a bit of damage was done. The water settled in the hollow of Water Street just before the bridge over the Bouquet River and then ran off the bridge into the river. Many homes had water in the cellars and at least one family had a great amount of sawdust from the icehouse left on their lawn.

At that time the new Grand Union was just being completed. Tile had just been laid on the floor but it was covered by so much water that it had to be replaced. The A&P store was flooded as was the post office, which was then located in an old brick building that still stands. There was also a diner right by the bridge, which has since been torn down.

This flood caused much excitement and damage to our village, but in a couple of weeks everything was back to normal except for the pond. The dam was never rebuilt, due to excessive insurance charges. Now it is just about filled in by trees and brush and one would never know a pretty body of water had been there.

We have had several other floods over the years but this one was the most unusual.

Water Street under water, July 1947

Married Life

$\mathcal{I}$ married Elverton Wrisley on July 19, 1947, in the Congregational Church in Elizabethtown with 100 guests present. My sister and brother were our attendants. The night before, during the rehearsal, we had a terrible thunderstorm. The lights went off and there we were in a dark church. Finally power came back on and we finished the rehearsal.

At the time there was no regular minister as one had left and they were searching for another. But I was pleased as it meant we could have a favorite Methodist minister who had given the benediction at my high school graduation. His name was Rev. Paul Thomas and he is now retired and living in Boca Raton, Florida.

Our reception was held at the Social Center. Cake, ice cream, and punch were served. After a trip to Maine we began housekeeping in a little house on River Street. We rented it from Elverton's parents. This house had been purchased from Sears, Roebuck years before. It came all pre-cut and numbered. Just had to be put together like a puzzle. There was even a fireplace in the living room. There were also two bedrooms, a dining room, kitchen, and bath. The house is still in good shape and used today, probably seventy years since it was built.

We lived there for four or five years and then decided to buy our own home. Our son, Calvin, was now almost three years old. We decided to buy a house on Cross Street that had been built in 1896. We liked it very much the first time we saw it and in three weeks we bought it and moved in. A small brook flows between the house and the one next to it. There were trout in it then but children loved to fish there so there are none now.

The house had been in very bad shape but the Barnetts from whom we bought it spent a whole summer renovating it, and new paper and paint were put in all the rooms. All we had to do was move in. Over the years we made other improvements, such as enlarging the living room, adding a new room, adding another bathroom, and putting a big, screened porch on the back. Also a garage was built along with a red barn for storage. Elverton's father and George Barnett's father took down a large carriage house at the home of Dr. Merrihew in Westport for lumber to build the garage.

When Calvin was ready to start kindergarten I had a chance to start teaching again in the second grade. So my son and I went to school together for thirteen years. I was his second grade teacher, which I enjoyed, but don't know if he did. I worked for eight more years until I retired in 1974, a year after my husband.

Maple Sugar Festivals

$\mathscr{I}$believe the first maple sugar festival held in Elizabethtown took place in 1957. I'm sure it was Mr. Harry MacDougal's idea. He was a great promoter of things to do in our town and he could carry his interest along to others who were willing to help. At the time he was president of the Adirondack Center Museum and this affair was held on its grounds and was a good way to earn money to keep it going.

Mr. MacDougal said he wanted the young folks to learn how syrup is made, so they brought the process out of the woods right into the village. First of all, the maple trees in the village had to be tapped, after receiving permission from the owners to do so. Sap was gathered from 450 village maple trees.

It takes forty gallons of sap to make a gallon of syrup, and it was reported that 150 gallons of syrup was made in 1957. The gathering of the sap was done by volunteers, and it was then taken to a modern sugar house on the Museum grounds. This sugar house was donated by Mr. and Mrs. J.D. Shattuck, summer residents who had made many gallons of syrup at their home on Hurricane Mountain.

The Festival was held on April 13th, 1957, with a very large crowd in attendance. The Lytle Family, a fine local band often seen on TV, furnished the music free of charge, and it was greatly enjoyed. One of the highlights of the day was being served a large plate of pancakes floating in the delicious syrup. Sausages and coffee were also served.

The first pint of maple syrup produced at the Elizabethtown sugar house was sent to then President Eisenhower. The second pint was sent to Governor Averell Harriman in Albany. Very gracious thank-you's were received from both men.

In 1960 the highlight of the festival was the appearance of Aunt Jemima. She was just great and enjoyed it as much as everyone else. Many pictures of her with local people were taken. I am pretty sure that her company furnished all the pancake flour for the pancakes.

It was a record crowd. Many of the men grew beards for this Festival and were dubbed "Brothers of the Brush." Besides the pancakes and sausages, many enjoyed the treat known as "sugar on snow" or Jack Wax, which is syrup that has been boiled to a high degree and then poured over packed snow. Mrs. Richard Lawrence had been saving three buckets of snow in her freezer for just this purpose. The syrup hardens and can be pulled off in strips. It's very sweet, of course, so many people have a sour pickle handy and then more sweet can be eaten.

One big pot of sap was kept hot for boiling eggs, which sold for ten cents and which tasted sweet with maple syrup through and through. There was also a beauty contest and a Festival Queen was chosen.

For some reason the festivals were stopped after 1963, probably because they were so much work for so many people. But now we have a wonderful Field, Forest and Stream Day in the fall. Each year the sugar house is put back into operation to show people how syrup is made.

Brian Carson

In August of 1957 another boy was born to Kay and Harlan Carson of Elizabethtown. His arrival was uneventful; no indication of what he would turn out to be—the foremost stunt car driver in the country. There were to be two more children, bringing the total to five, but Brian was the only one who turned to stunt driving.

His parents and I graduated from high school together and were the best of friends. When Brian was ready for second grade, he was not assigned to the class that I taught. I was always sorry as it would be great now to claim to have been his second grade teacher. One brother and one sister did go through my room, however.

Even before he was old enough for a driver's license, Brian was practicing here at home smashing bicycles, motorcycles, and cars. He built a ramp and would hit it at top speed and fly through the air, landing in the road or a field. He enlisted help for his stunts from other boys his age. For the most part they were eager to help, but were very secretive about the whole thing because they knew that if their parents found out, everything would come to a screeching halt.

Brian was known as "Crazy Carson" here at home, but that name was dropped as soon as he left Elizabethtown in 1974 and began to hit the big shows. After leaving here, he joined the Joie Chitwood Thrill Show where he worked for about eight years. Then he formed his own business called Action Events.

After many shows around the country, in July of 1988 he decided to put on a show near Elizabethtown for his friends and relatives. The stunt, which he performed in a stadium in Plattsburgh, was to drive his car up a ramp at sixty miles an hour and hit four cars piled on top of each other which were also loaded with explosives. This was his fourth time doing this particular stunt and he was pleased with the way it turned out.

After it was over he said he was okay but that the pain would set in by the next morning. Over the years he has had more broken bones than he can count, but it doesn't stop him.

Brian performed the above stunt before a crowd of 80,000 people at Anaheim Stadium in California and received a standing ovation. Later he performed the same stunt at the Charlotte, North Carolina, Motor Speedway where he was shaken up but not injured. He zoomed up the ramp at 70 m.p.h. into flames four stories high. He was supposed to land right side up but landed upside down on parked cars.

Today I think we should be proud of Brian for his great stunts before probably a million people who have really enjoyed his shows. And to think he started out in this small town. He has performed in many cities across the country and in Europe, and has been in several movies and on television several times.

Brian knew exactly what he wanted to do in his life and he did it, regardless of bad accidents, broken bones, and not knowing how the day would end. He has one more stunt he wants to do—that is to jump off a motel roof eighteen stories in the air onto a parking lot. Time will tell about this wild idea.

My Father and His Cars

$\mathcal{M}$y father, Logan Phinney, once reminisced for a newspaper reporter about the cars he had bought, traded, and driven since his first Model T. These were his memories in 1976, when he was 85 years old:

"The Model T was the first one I had—that was in 1916. That was a pick-up, and a couple of years later I went back and traded for a touring car. I paid $435 for that car.

"You'd drive a car just as fast as it would go and that would save a lot on the pounding. If the road was washboardy, by going fast you'd miss a lot of the humps. Yes, we always put the cars up in the winter. We'd take the tires off and put them down cellar. Course they couldn't sand the roads like they do now on account of the sleighing, you know.

"I was thinking the other day about the Egglefields and all the other dealers. They had to go to Buffalo after the cars, you know. I think I went out there three times for the Egglefields. It was a hard trip.

"That was in old Bert's time. Harrison and Spencer had a finger in it—Harrison was the mechanic. Well, they'd ask four or five of us fellows to go...and they'd put you on a train down at Westport. It was the sleeper at night but you sat up all the way to Buffalo.

"You'd get into Buffalo at daylight, they'd give you breakfast, and then you'd go right over to the factory. Those cars would come down on endless belts—I remember that—and when you got your quota you'd start for Elizabethtown.

"There wasn't too much stopping. Sometimes they'd run pretty good and then sometimes there was bound to be a little trouble. And Harrison—he was a young fella then—he'd hurry up and patch 'em up and just as quick as he got one rolling Harrison would yell, 'Push her, push her!' So we'd push 'em."

My father talked about how they used to convert Model T's for wintertime use. "Harry Sayre and Billy Ellsworth used to put a track right around the front wheels and the back wheels and they could go anywhere with them. They was both mail-carriers.

"Why, you could do anything with those old Model T's. I bought a saw rig and standard and I used a pulley that Gilbert Taylor made for me and I'd jack up the back wheel and saw all my wood with the old Model T."

He also talked about trading cars: "I remember I traded once with the Bronson boys over in Stowersville. I went through there one day and I traded and got a Ford. It was a high, enclosed car. Well, my goodness, I was driving it home and it worked all right, till I got going down the hill into Lewis. I come down that hill there and I heard the darned rear end giving out. And it went out. Well, I got down to Albert Sergeant's sawmill there and I backed right up to a sawdust pile there, took out that little plug you put the grease in, and stuffed it full of sawdust. Well, yes, it went right along then. Well, I drove into Lewis and right up to Harry Johnson's.

"Well, he had an old pickup truck that Louis Lesperance had and it set right there. I visited with Harry and I told him, 'I'd like to get a pick-up truck, Harry.' 'Well, he says, 'There's one right there.' Well anyway we traded right there. I see him a few days after and Harry said, 'I didn't know you worked anywheres near a sawmill!'"

My Life After the Working Years

𝒯he "Golden Years" arrived too soon. You look forward to them while you are busy working toward them and all of a sudden they are upon you. I had taught school twenty-nine years, my husband was retired, so why shouldn't I try it?

To date I have had twenty years of busy, happy retirement. We did a great deal of traveling at first. Hawaii was very enjoyable, Florida a few times, five trips to California—two by airplane, one by train, one by bus, and an earlier one by car—and then a trip to England.

Since my husband passed away in 1989, I have still kept our home and live in it with my son, Calvin, which is very nice for me. My days are filled with meetings—church, Garden Club, library, and Eastern Star.

I do enjoy cooking very much and love to have folks in for a meal. My collection of over 400 cookbooks is very enjoyable to read, but not always to use. We have a rather large garden, which means work.

One hobby that has taken a great deal of time is my scrapbook collection. It was started in 1940 with newspaper clippings of local interest and it continues to the present time. About ninety large books are filled with very interesting articles which have been enjoyed by many people.

As people say who have retired, "I don't know how I had the time to work."

Marilyn Cross

$\mathcal{M}$y name is Marilyn Hathaway Cross. I was born in 1930 and have lived in Lewis all my life with the exception of three years in the Elizabethtown and Wadhams area. I have a husband, John, one daughter, one granddaughter, and two great-grandchildren as well as four stepchildren and six stepgrandchildren.

I have done a variety of work and always looked at each different job as a challenge. My last positions were Nutrition Teaching Assistant for the Cooperative Extension and program director for a senior center.

My First Home

$\mathcal{I}$grew up in a small four-room log house on Wells Hill, which was Rev. Cyrus Comstock's home 100 years before we lived there. Father Comstock was the founder of the Lewis Congregational Church and invented the Comstock buckboard wagon.

By the time we moved in about 1930 the logs had been covered over on the outside with clapboards and on the inside with plaster covered with wallpaper. We never worried about the cold as we were always warm or didn't know any different.

We had to prepare for winter. No one had ever heard of storm windows. We cut rag strips and used a silver knife to crowd the strips into the cracks around the windows to keep out the cold. We also "banked" the house with leaves on the outside. This probably helped to keep the floors warm.

We had a Home Comfort cookstove in the kitchen and a small chunk stove in the living room. This stove had a big door and held a large chunk of wood that would burn all night. All water was heated on the kitchen stove, which had a reservoir that held several gallons of water. We had to go to the well for water, but when I was about five years old we acquired the luxury of a pitcher pump in the kitchen. We had no worry about water pipes freezing and we always had a full wood box.

The large pantry had lots of shelves to set the pans of milk on. There were several large barrels for storage of sugar and flour for the winter. Hams and rolls of sausage were hung on the porch or in the woodshed in the winter.

The woodshed was on the back of the house and everyone had to work to fill it for winter. Getting the wood was a year-round project. At an early age I could keep up with anyone on a two-man crosscut saw. There is a trick to making the saw go smooth and not catch. I also used a bucksaw and ranked wood. Putting up the high ranks of wood was an art. If you didn't keep it even and straight, by the time you had a rank over your

Me and my brother in front of our Wells Hill home

Shep, the dog that came to stay

head it could fall over. Once the woodshed was filled we had a big feeling of satisfaction and we could move on to the many other preparations for winter.

The porch was on three sides of the house with the woodshed at the end, then the privy with the three holes. The holes were of graded heights to accommodate the family members. A lot of people referred to the privy as "papa, mama and baby bear," or "going to visit Mrs. Jones."

The large porch of the house held many items necessary for our survival. The north porch next to the woodshed was home for the icebox, the large sit-down separator, the metal shoe last, the crank-wheel washing machine, crank wringers, the washtub stand, and two big washtubs. We always rinsed our clothes twice. All socks had to be turned inside out in the first rinse tub. We always washed dish towels in the first load. Underwear, socks, and overalls were washed last in order of color. We always used blueing in our rinse water.

The clothespin bag hung on the porch wall. In summer birds often nested in the bag but we never disturbed the nest. We would put our clothes over the line without pins or put them on the green grass to whiten the white clothes. This was before Clorox or bleach.

The front porch and the south side porch each had a swing and several chairs where we could sit and watch the rain or entertain neighbors, friends, and relatives. Dahlias were planted along the front porch and continued for about fifty feet along the edge of our long driveway. There were several handles along the back of the porch where boards could be lifted to disclose a nesting or laying hen. My father soon did away with that and used the hen house.

My father put hinges on the top of the second step on the stair going up to our two bedrooms. The step opened up to store overshoes and mittens. We had very little storage space. My clothes closet was an area under a chimney about fourteen inches square and four feet high. The old stovepipes ran all over the house from the stove to the chimney. They helped to heat the house but were dangerous and chimney fires were common.

We used kerosene lamps. Every room had a lamp table and nothing but the kerosene lamp could be put on that table. The kitchen had a bracket lamp on the wall over the table beside the clock shelf. Just inside the pantry door was the wall-mounted coffee grinder.

By 1940 we had a Delco system with thirty-six batteries. We now had electricity if we could put up with the noise of the engine that charged the batteries. This Delco system took up a large area of the cellar under the stairs where there was a sturdy table with two shelves holding the batteries. Electricity came to Wells Hill about 1948, two years after we moved from the hill.

The cellar also had a huge wooden potato bin, an apple box, a large box for carrots, squash, and onions, and shelves on two sides for the canned goods. We pulled house plants and hung them in the cellar for the winter. We had another wooden box for dahlia and gladiola bulbs. We couldn't forget the box of garden soil to start our tomato plants in mid-winter as well as the pork and cider barrels.

This house was built for the times and was very comfortable for those days. We didn't have to worry about pipes freezing, a bad storm that would cause us to lose our lights and heat, or being snowbound and unable to get to town. We didn't have many clothes so we had enough storage space.

The radio and Zane Grey books were our only luxury, our prized possessions. We always had enough food to take us to the next gardening season, so we never went to town in the winter. The mail was no concern as all we ever got was a Montgomery Ward catalog or an order. A little later we sub-scribed to the *Grit* paper and always read "Hank and Min Crabb."

We would find it impossible to live in a house with no con-veniences today but we really didn't know any different then. Our home was our castle.

Growing Up in Lewis

$\mathscr{G}$rowing up on Wells Hill in the town of Lewis in the 1930s and '40s was much different than the lives of children who grew up in Elizabethtown. Elizabethtown was only five miles away but it could have been 500.

When I left the little elementary school in Lewis and entered seventh grade in Elizabethtown in 1943, I had never used a telephone. There were only about six in our area. We also didn't have electricity because the lines didn't go to Wells Hill. I knew how to light the lantern to go to the barn and I could milk and feed the calf without having the buckets kicked over. I knew how to clean the lamps and lanterns and trim the wicks and fill them with kerosene. This was a daily project.

I also knew how to care for sick animals. We often took a small or sick piglet to the house to try to save it. We would line the big metal washtub with warm blankets and warm wrapped rocks to keep the pig warm. We would give the little pig warm drinks. The piglet was often a small one or the runt of the litter and couldn't survive at first in its big family. Sometimes this loving care and home doctoring was successful if the baby hadn't been injured before being discovered.

The collie dog that was dropped at the nearby Hamilton-Milholland home in Lewis became a member of our family in 1936, when my brother was one year old and just starting to walk. Miss Veda Milholland and Miss Margaret Hamilton searched to find the owner of this beautiful dog but no one ever came forth to claim him. After several months of advertising the lost dog and paying a local man named Jack Hood for the dog's room and board they decided it was time for Shep to have a permanent home.

Shep was an important member of our family until his death of old age in 1945. No dog would ever take the place of old Shep. My mother was not a lover of animals but she was the one who brought Shep into our lives and she never once said anything against him. I was starting school at this time and my brother and Shep were always together. My brother loved to hide behind trees but Shep's tail was always seen waving. I don't think my brother ever knew that Shep always gave him away. My mother let him think he was well hidden. Our cats usually stayed at the barn but Shep always had a favorite that followed him to the house for nap time. Many afternoons found two kids, a dog, and a cat asleep in a heap on the porch.

Growing up in Lewis was a farm life and the animals were our playmates. The Elizabethtown classmates had the Social Center, movie theater, diner, hospital, and churches close enough to attend as well as having friends nearby. Our nearest neighbor was about one mile away. Elizabethtown seemed like a big scary place to me. They had the big hotels where people were able to work. It was too far for most people from Lewis to travel to in those days. Growing up in Lewis was a hard struggle for survival and Elizabethtown always appeared better off financially.

I feel people from both towns missed something. The farm life was an education in survival but the town life was a different education. The residents of Elizabethtown had the opportunity to learn that there was a better way of life.

Evenings Without Electricity

$\mathcal{I}$ grew up using kerosene lamps. When I was about eleven years old my father put in a Delco system to provide electricity, but we didn't use it often since the engine to run the system made so much noise and gave off fumes. So we still used kerosene lamps.

I can remember going to visit homes where there was always a person sitting in the corner in the dark. Many people didn't have electricity or water until the late 1940s. People didn't miss what they never had and really didn't know what these conveniences could do for them.

We always had our evening meal early to try to get the dishes and things cleaned up before dark. Then after doing the dishes all the buckets and pans had to be filled with water from the well or spring for morning.

Schoolwork had to be done as soon as we got home from school and I could never handle that as I had to unwind after my day at school. I usually worked on the wood and then it was time to eat, do the dishes, and clean up. By then it was too dark to do schoolwork by lamplight, and we couldn't do much close work, like reading, by lamplight, either. Often the homework was done bright and early the next morning.

We usually played dominoes, chess, Chinese checkers, or put puzzles together. We always wore out the new Montgomery Ward catalog looking at it and wishing. A new catalog was an awaited event as we could get the old one and cut paper dolls or paste the pictures in a scrapbook using our homemade paste of flour and water. While we played my mother would go back to the kitchen and prepare a snack. It could be fudge or popcorn or my father might crack butternuts. The snack on Sunday night was always popcorn. We had crackers and milk for Sunday night supper so we could eat a bushel of popped corn.

On weekend nights we could stay up after nine o'clock, so in the winter we went ice skating on the Mill Pond. There were always people of all ages and we had plenty of supervision. Many of us had the old skates that clamped on our boots; later came the shoe skates, a wonderful improvement. We always had a big bonfire and a great time. Other nights we could go sliding.

We lived by the term, "Work from daylight to dark," and usually we were in bed a very short time after dark. We had more fun in the winter when the days were shorter and we didn't work as hard. The summers also meant work from daylight to dark, but the days were long and we were ready for bed by dark with no time for fun.

Home Remedies

$\mathcal{I}$n the old days we had to rely on home remedies for most of our ailments. I really think the old-timers thought if something tasted terrible it would cure anything.

The winter season always brought the small basin on the back of the stove filled with a butter, vinegar, molasses, and onion mix, sometimes called onion syrup or sulfur and molasses. We were to take a teaspoonful of this hot syrup several times a day.

How I hated orange juice—the only time we ever got it was with a dose of castor oil. I remember one time my mother asked me if I wanted a glass of orange juice and I said, "No! You will put that stuff in it." She finally let me inspect the juicer and glass and I said, "Okay." I can remember carefully taking a tiny sip to be sure. I had castor oil in my juice too many times to take any chances.

We gathered catnip and hung it in the woodshed to dry for the winter. We were given catnip tea or lemonade as a hot drink to fight a cold.

I always had a cold and earache all winter. A remedy for earache was a cloth bag filled with warm salt. My mother had two salt bags so while one was heating in the warming oven I had to lie with the other one over my ear. Then when that one got cold the other one would be ready to use. Occasionally she put a drop of warm sweet oil in my ear. Then she would grease my chest with warm Save the Baby ointment and cover it with a heated flannel cloth. Boy, did I ever smell!

I really believe now that my problem was allergies. We burned wood at home and our schoolhouse also had a big woodstove. Once I started going to school in Elizabethtown where there was a furnace my problems were less. We were still burning wood at home, though. I now know I am allergic to woodsmoke, but no one ever thought of allergies in those days. Just suffered it out, and I did!

Cloverline Salve was often sold by children. How I loved the pictures they gave as a bonus for buying the salve. I usually got to choose the picture. Save the Baby came from the store in a small glass bottle. I think Vicks came later. There was also a horrible black salve called Iodex.

There was a Hardy Salve that was a hard lump that we softened in a tin cup on the stove. It possibly came from a tree like our spruce gum. It was used for healing cuts and drawing out slivers. We always had a hot water bottle or heated a rock as a hot pack for injuries, aches, and pains. Our ice pack was ice chipped off the big block and wrapped in a wash cloth—no plastic.

If none of these remedies brought relief the doctor would be called. There was Dr. Gersen, Dr. Goff, and Dr. Kunz. I believe Dr. Kunz was used more by the older people. He was the last doctor to live and practice in the Town of Lewis. Dr. Gersen was in Elizabethtown and Dr. Goff in Keene. My earliest knowledge was that Dr. Goff charged two dollars for a house call and one dollar for an office visit.

Saturday Night

$\mathcal{S}$aturday nights were always a planned event in the 1930s and '40s. We worked hard all week so we could enjoy our weekend. Everyone worked from daylight to dark. In the summer we had gardening, haying, and canning. We picked hundreds of quarts of strawberries, raspberries, blackberries, and blueberries. The big meal always included a pie or side dish of berries.

In the winter we cut the wood to heat our home. I hurried home from school to get at the work as I knew it had to be done. Night and morning brought milking and barn chores. I learned to milk at an early age and was always anxious to get the first quart of milk to feed the many barn cats yelling for their meal.

Then Saturday morning my first duty was to do the churning and make the butter. I always disliked churning as the handle would come out of the churn and be hard to push back in. It took about an hour of churning to get to butter. I was always the first to get a glass of buttermilk.

We milked earlier on Saturday night to get a little extra time for the weekend. After milking, the milk had to be separated. Then I had the job of washing the separator with the dozens of tiny parts that had to be put back together in perfect order. After the work was all done we could start for Grandma's and our weekend. No one ever left home without putting everything in order. Dishes and housework were always finished before any pleasure.

My father would drop my mother, brother, and myself off at her mother's. My mother's sisters would also meet there. The men would take off for Burpee's store to sit around the old pot-bellied stove and tell tales.

The women all sat around my grandmother's big dining room table to sew the material that we used to make rag rugs. She had a beautiful big kerosene hanging lamp over the table so everyone preferred to meet there, since the light was better than at the other houses. No one had electricity or bathrooms. We always had snacks and something different every week. Sometimes fudge, apples, cookies, donuts, popcorn and sometimes something special like an orange or peach or pear.

When I was young I liked to play with my grandmother's button box while the grown-ups sat around the table sewing carpet rags. I started sewing rags and making quilts at an early age. These Saturday nights around the dining room table were a time of generations being together with the older influencing the lives of the younger ones.

My father would pick us up about nine o'clock and we would start home. The distance was about half a mile and often the old car would blow a fuse and we would go home with no headlights. There really wasn't any danger as no one else was ever on the road at this time of night.

After a night of sleep and doing the morning chores we were ready for Sunday and a day of rest. We usually visited other relatives on Sunday afternoon or had a family picnic.

After World War II our lives started to change, and Saturday nights brought square dances and fewer family activities. Ice skating still remained a winter favorite but making rugs and quilts was not popular. I remember my first store-bought blanket and it was a precious item. No more old homemade quilts and rugs.

A Way of Survival

In the 1930s there were a lot of people doing a variety of jobs to make a living and provide the items necessary for survival. There were no frills.

The meat truck came but I don't think my mother bought much, as we raised pigs, chickens, and beef. My father was a hunter and we had venison. Deer were abundant and we often saw several at a time in our yard. The men who came with the meat wagon were Hardy Talbot, Alfred LaRue, and Joe McGee.

Frank and Analita Stevens operated the store in Lewis after Ralph Nichols gave it up. Willis and Mildred Dickerson came when the Stevenses moved to Elizabethtown and opened the drug store. This store had a soda fountain, and the Stevenses had a delivery service. Mrs. Stevens bought live chickens and hens from my father. She killed and dressed them in the back of the store.

Bessie Cutting repaired watches and clocks at her home on the Muzzy Road in Lewis. Anything that couldn't be repaired with a cup of kerosene and a feather was taken to Bessie.

Lulu Nichols sold a cleaning powder like Spic 'n Span that was called Uka, and a pink clay-like compound in a can for cleaning wallpaper.

Willard Clark in Elizabethtown was where everyone went for all bicycle problems or to buy a used bike. Automobiles were not the complicated vehicles of today and everyone did their own repairs or went to Johnson's garage in Lewis.

Charlie Warren was the shoe cobbler in Elizabethtown and he could sew and repair our shoes if my father couldn't do it.

There was an iceman who delivered to the people who couldn't cut their own. My father always cut and put up the ice for our use. Many homes had an ice house. Bob Sweatt and Raymond Hyde sold ice.

Since this was hard times, there were always men walking with their backpacks selling small items like needles. Sometimes a hobo came along. Once you gave a hobo a good feed he marked a sign for others, so if we saw one coming my mother locked the door and we hid. My mother was afraid of strangers.

Then we had the ragman, who we looked forward to all year. When we cut up old clothes for rugs and quilts, we saved the scraps and put them in a burlap bag. Once the bag was full we tied it up and took it to the ice house and hung it up high on a nail so the mice and squirrels didn't get into it. In the spring when the ragman came, we had five or six bags to trade. He would weigh them and show my mother his wares. She would select needles and thread for her next winter's work. Sometimes she owed him a few pennies and other times he paid her.

There was a milkman who went door-to-door but we had our own milk. We had several customers who came with their pails after milk in the 1930s. Then along came pasteurization and government laws. But by the time the laws were enforced it was easier to find work and not be as dependent on the land.

Theron Lobdell sharpened ice skates. Several people sold Larkin products, which were things like shampoo and toilet water. Everyone had a Larkin desk. An occasional Rawleigh man stopped. He sold spices, home remedies, liniments, and cough syrup.

Often people would just stop by for a chat or on their way from berry picking for a drink of water. Nearly everyone picked wild berries of all kinds for their families to use and to trade or sell for a little needed cash.

There was lots of open land and people could go cross-lot instead of the long way around. When people came to visit it was to stay all day, often for both noon and night meals. You never popped in and out. That would have been an insult.

My mother was a dressmaker and often did this for extra money or trade. People used their feed bags to make clothes.

Several farmers including my family sold or traded milk, butter, eggs, cottage cheese, maple syrup, and chickens to private customers. Butter and eggs were exchanged for groceries at Burpee's store. In 1890 the history books said the country store was a dying breed, but the country store continued in Lewis for 100 years after that prediction. The farmers selling items didn't seem to hurt the store's other business.

We can't forget John Dickerson, then the Bronson boys, coming to do the plowing with a horse or two. They plowed all day and had dinner with us at noon. My father plowed about five acres of our twenty-eight-acre farm.

Alec Gelina was an old man who lived about two or three miles past our house and walked to town a couple of times a year. He talked with a French accent and my brother was terrified of him.

The 1940s brought the Hathaway and McPhail families to a house up the road from us. They often stopped by. Then the Christmas season brought their annual house guest, the well-known Adirondack hermit Noah John Rondeau, who often walked past our house on his way to town and stopped to chat.

The Gypsies came every summer. It was a sight to see them pull in with many wagons, horses, cows, and chickens. Some people walking, others riding. They camped where the Ruth Stringham house was built. In the '30s that area was a beautiful clearing with trees for shade and a perfect spot to camp. There was an excellent well there for their needs.

There was a Gypsy girl about my age and a boy about two years older. Since my grandmother lived next door, we played together. They came over and I was fascinated with their lifestyles and asked questions, but never got much of an answer. Where did they come from? Where were they going? Why? They would give no answer. The only thing I ever knew is that they lived in a tent and their mother and grandmother told fortunes. Everyone thought the Gypsies stole but my grandmother never lost anything. People always said, "Lock your henhouse or the Gypsies will get your chickens," and that they stole children.

There were many places in this area where the Gypsies camped, always near a good water supply. We never knew when they would come or when they would leave. We played together one night and the next morning they were gone. We had no idea they were leaving. I feel the Gypsies followed the seasons, and weather probably played a big part in their lives.

Their style was much like our modern-day gypsies with their elaborate motor homes and red pickup trucks. These people in the '30s were traveling with horses and tents even though cars had come into our lives. For me as a small child they were of a different time.

When they returned the next year the boy and girl were with them again but didn't come to visit us. We had to stay near the house and not go near the Gypsy camp. Probably my mother kept her watchful eye on us all the time they were around. I never dared to say it but I longed all year for the Gypsies to return and seeing them come up the road was a thrill for me. We had little else for excitement in our lives in the '30s.

Gypsies come to town!

Dish Time

$\mathscr{I}$t is almost impossible to realize what a job it was to wash dishes when I was growing up. I can't understand the young people today saying they don't like to do dishes when they have hot running water and liquid soap.

My mother and I had to make sure the reservoir on the stove and the tea kettles were filled so we would have hot water. That often meant several trips outside to the pitcher pump.

We always did the dishes immediately after every meal. We had a sink in a dark corner where we could wash the dishes in the daytime. But the dishes from the evening meal had to be done by the light of the bracket lamp so that meant setting the pans on the kitchen table.

We had soap scraps in a soap saver—a metal cage with a handle that we shook to try to make suds. This wasn't too great so when liquid soap came along we thought that was the best.

We were taught to wash glasses first, then silver, plates, and pans last. We always had to rinse in boiling water and wipe the dishes and put them on the pantry shelves in the proper places.

As we conserved everything, the dishwater was used to water the flowers along the driveway. Then the dishpans were wiped and hung on the clothesline on the back porch.

Then came the separator with all the pieces to be washed with no soap and rinsed. Everything used for the separator had to be clean and fresh towels had to be used and a special pan to wash the parts.

We then checked the rain tub to be sure it was in place to catch rainwater.

I think older people enjoy doing dishes now and having good suds and instant hot water. It was a hard task years ago.

The Hens Aren't Laying

$\mathcal{M}$y father would say, "If the hens can't pay their way we can't keep them. We will see what happens next week."

There is a time of year when hens stop laying eggs and it is several months before they start again. It always seemed as if my father wanted them to start laying again soon so we would not have to go through the two days it took to get the hens canned. But the canning always had to be done.

The day before, my mother would start bringing the wide-mouth quart jars upstairs to wash, and would check to be sure she had rings and lids or jar rubbers. She always planned to do seven or fourteen hens as her canner took seven quarts.

Early the next morning my father caught the hens and cut their heads off with an axe on a wooden cutting block. He always saved a wing so we had a new whisk broom. Then he hung the hens on the clothesline to bleed.

By this time the water was boiling in the big iron pot that hung on a tripod over the open fire. My father dunked one chicken at a time in the pot and pulled off most of the feathers. My mother and I cleaned off what feathers he missed. Then we took them to the house, where the table was ready with cutting boards covered with a dozen layers of newspaper.

Mother and I started dressing them out. Then my father took them and cut them into pieces. There were seven pans with ice water to cool the chickens. One chicken was put in each pan and fresh ice water was added every few hours.

The next morning my mother sterilized the jars and packed one chicken in each quart jar. Everyone said it was impossible to get a full cut-up hen in any quart jar. She had a system for the wide-mouth quarts but it didn't work on the regular quarts. After packing the chicken in the jar, she filled the jar with water and one teaspoon of salt and sealed it.

The wood stove was already going and there was plenty of hot water for the canner. She put the seven quarts in the water bath canner and boiled them for three hours. This meant the wood stove had to have a hot fire, so the chickens were usually done in the late fall when the weather was colder. If they had fourteen hens for one day that meant about eight hours for the two loads. She only had one canner as only one would fit on the stove at one time.

The next morning, or the fourth day after my mother had brought the cans up from cellar, the seven or fourteen jars full of chicken were carried back to the cellar and placed on the shelf for one winter's food supply.

We never had chicken to eat during the days this was going on. I was sure glad of that.

Winter is Coming

$\mathcal{P}$reparation for winter was a year-round project when I was growing up on Wells Hill in Lewis. We only had the car licensed for six months of the year, from June to December. This meant that everything heavy had to be purchased before the end of December.

My mother had a large pantry with big barrels for flour and sugar, which were purchased in 100-pound cloth bags. This meant we had material for new dish towels and to make sausage bags. I learned to sew in about 1938 on a treadle sewing machine, making bags to put our homemade sausage in.

There was a big box upstairs where my mother kept her baking soda and baking powder. She always bought about a dozen boxes of baking soda because it was used for other purposes than baking. It was a famous medical necessity, used to soothe burns and wounds and reduce a fever.

We gathered several bushels of butternuts and walnuts. We gathered lots of apples to fill the large bin in the cellar. The poorer apples went into a big iron kettle in the yard and were cooked for the pigs along with squash, pumpkins, potatoes, and other surplus food from the gardens. Another huge box held carrots and beets while a larger one held potatoes. Bags of onions and catnip hung from the beams.

There were hundreds of jars of canned goods on the shelves. A bushel of peas or corn would fill seven pint jars. It took all summer to fill about 300 jars of chicken, peas, corn, rhubarb, fruits, pickles, beef, venison, tomatoes, and mincemeat. There always were several crocks filled with salt pork. The hams and rolls of sausage were hung in the woodshed. The beef and venison were usually canned.

It took a lot of planning to survive the winters. The firewood had to be ready for winter as we were dependent on our supply of wood to heat the house. Getting the wood was almost a year-round project. We also had to have our winter supply of kerosene for our lamps and to start the wood fires. The house-cleaning had to be finished and cracks filled to keep out the cold winter air.

The winter was long and we were often snowbound for several days at a time, but the snowplows always opened the roads as soon as they could with their antique equipment. We didn't have any fear about being snowbound as this was the way it had to be at that time. Possibly I had no fear because I was a child, since now I get uneasy if our telephone is out of order or we can't get our driveway plowed. I never felt isolated as a child or had any fear. We always had plenty of food to weather out the storm.

Bucksaw competition, 1949

It's a Cold Winter

*W*hen I was growing up, the winters were much colder than they are now. They were so cold that soon after Thanksgiving hams and sausage rolls were hung on the porch where they stayed frozen. We would bring them in the house, cut off a piece for a meal, and take the meat back to the porch. This was before anyone had freezers.

Clothing was for protection from the cold weather. Nearly everyone wore long underwear or the one-piece union suit. The union suits came in all sizes. They were similar to the stretch suits infants wear today, but ours had a drop seat for bathroom purposes. The girls wore long, brown stockings over their long underwear. It was nearly impossible to get the stockings over the underwear and not have wrinkles.

Winter rules in Elizabethtown

Ski suits were worn by everyone. There were no zippers, only large buttons. Jackets were usually double-breasted and made of heavy, picky wool. Like the ski pants, they absorbed lots of snow and kept us dry. Hats, mittens, and scarves were always worn.

The footgear wasn't that great. We wore heavy socks, shoes, and rubber overshoes to keep us dry. Even though we were warm everywhere else, our feet were often cold. The rubber overshoes made our feet sweat but they still got cold.

It was often 25 or 30 degrees below zero. People had to walk long distances, and schoolrooms were not comfortable. There were a few cars but many didn't have any heaters, and if there was one it often wasn't much good.

After World War II, however, our clothing began to improve in style and comfort.

The Old Mill Pond

𝒯he old mill pond in Lewis was an important part of our lives in the past. The Loyal Marshall mill, later known as the Craig Garvey Mill, was located on the bank of the lower mill pond just after you turn east from Route 9 toward the Northway. The bridge is still there but the pond is now gone. In the old days the logs were dumped into the pond on their journey to the sawmill.

The summer brought us to the ponds and the falls that were our favorite fishing spots. There were cranberries in the upper mill pond and many families went out in boats and gathered them to make cranberry sauce to complement their Thanksgiving and Christmas dinners. The pond was abundant with waterlilies and the edges were aglow with beautiful blue and yellow iris.

Sometime between Thanksgiving and Christmas the ice in the pond was safe for skating. We could never go on the upper mill pond as we were told there were air holes and it was dangerous. But the lower mill pond was all we needed for a good time.

Skating was a favorite evening of fun. The temperature was sometimes 20 degrees below zero on a cold, crisp evening but we would often have as many as twenty adults and children sitting on their sleds or skating around the warm fire. We were always able to get old tires to burn to keep warm and to give us enough light to see where we were skating.

Many of us had skates that clamped onto our shoes. It was impossible to skate very far before they fell off and we had to start over again, but we never gave up. I think I was about 15 when I got my first skates attached to boots. That was a great improvement.

The mill pond supplied water for Martha Wade's cow. They cut a hole in the ice in a corner for the cow to drink, and Henry Toby led the cow down the road to the water hole. Nellie

Marble had a hole on the northeast channel for her animals to drink.

There was another area of the pond where the men cut ice to fill their ice houses. They started cutting when the ice was twelve to fourteen inches thick; they cut it into blocks. It was almost a community event as several families in town got together and contributed to the cutting and filling of several ice houses. The ice was necessary as this was before electric refrigerators and families used an icebox to keep their food cool.

The old mill pond was not only used for recreation but was necessary for survival many years ago. Everyone seemed to have their spot on the pond and were respectful of other people who used the pond for their needs.

The pond is no longer there but the trickling brook still flows where the center of the pond was located. The iris have been crowded out and there is no longer a dam to hold the water in the pond. But the memories of the old mill pond live on in the minds of many older people.

A Christmas Surprise

*C*hristmas was an exciting time at our house. This was when we got new stockings, mittens, socks, crayons, paper, pencils, and other necessary items. My mother's family made and bought things all year, planning for a big Christmas. We went to my grandmother's for the tree on Christmas Eve and opened gifts from my aunts. There was always plenty of candy. We were pleased with all the new things.

We had to hurry home after the tree to get to bed and wait for Santa Claus. We would be up early the next morning for the things Santa had left in our stockings. My stocking was a big, white cheesecloth one that had belonged to my mother when she was a little girl. We had trinkets and candy in our stockings and I always had a doll and my brother had a toy truck or car.

After the tree, my father would take the milk pail and go to the barn. One year when he opened the door, he came back in saying, "Look here! Santa forgot to bring this in." He had a shiny, new sled. Later I heard him and my mother talking and they were trying to figure out who drove down our long, snowy driveway and left the sled. Everyone he suspected denied leaving it. So we knew Santa Claus had left the sled. It has been well over fifty years and we never knew who left us the shiny, new Flexible Flyer.

After a few trips down the hill on our new sled we went back to my grandmother's for a Christmas dinner of chicken and biscuits, squash, cranberry sauce, and pumpkin and apple pie with homemade ice cream. Everything for the dinner was grown by family members or gathered wild. The cranberries came from the upper mill pond in Lewis. My aunt went out in a boat to gather them. About the only things from the store were flour, sugar, and spices. We always gathered nuts and apples. The nuts were in our homemade fudge for Christmas and the apples made our pies and applesauce.

I don't remember having turkey for Christmas or Thanksgiving until I was grown and went back home. I don't know if it was too expensive or just not available here.

When I was growing up, Christmas was a happy time for our family. We had lots of gifts and never once realized they were necessary items that many other families got when school started in September. The only gifts that were not necessary items were my doll and my brother's truck. I still have the sled Santa left many years ago.

If You Need it, Make it

In my early life our needs were very few, and we really didn't have any wants. If we needed something my father would go down to his shop and find the materials to make it with. When I was a baby he made my stroller for summer and a sleigh for the winter. As I got older he built me a playhouse with two windows. He made me a doll bed and table from scrap wood and made chairs and cupboards from slabs. He even made a trough for the pigs to eat from. He also made my mother several cupboards.

On a rainy day he would get the shoe last ready with the proper size foot and put on new soles. The sewing and work on our shoes that he couldn't do went to Charlie Warren in Elizabethtown. My father patched our rubbers and overshoes and the inner tubes for tires.

If the milk pail or a pan leaked he would repair it with a Mendit—a small metal patch that screwed on. Then the pan was as good as new until it needed another patch. There was never an end to repairing sap buckets with Mendits. There were a few wooden sap buckets around but by the time I can remember we used the metal ones.

My mother made everything last forever. She was always darning socks or patching clothes. She often cut cardboard to put in our shoes or slippers. She made soap and cooked all kinds of food from scratch. There were no prepared mixes then. If we needed a quilt she made it. She made all our clothes and made them last forever. Most of the fabric was flour sacks or grain bags.

Once in awhile our "rich" cousins from Vermont would come over loaded with clothes from their three daughters and sometimes a piece of furniture. My father and mother always repaid them with produce from our huge gardens.

One of the highlights of my life was when my mother had some plissé or seersucker material and surprised me with three new nightgowns with wide crocheted necks and shoulders. I have always been partial to nice nightgowns.

My first memory of a nice dress-up outfit was when I was about twelve years old. My mother worked one day a week for the Milhollands, who lived a few miles from our house in the big place that is now the Meadowmount music school. Miss Veda Milholland, who was a singer, gave my mother a beautiful red velvet riding suit. My mother made me a skirt and jacket from that material.

Miss Veda Milholland's sister, Miss Inez Milholland, was a famous suffragist who had died of leukemia when she was only thirty-three years old. I have been told the red velvet riding suit was what Miss Inez Milholland wore when she rode her white horse in parades. I really think today I would prefer to see the riding suit in the museum but at that time the beautiful

My mother and father, Lottie and William
Hathaway

red velvet outfit my mother made me was an example of how people made use of everything.

At that time our stores didn't carry any wants, just our basic needs. Each family took care of their needs from something they had on hand. So if anyone needed anything, they made it and made it last forever. I don't think wants came into our lives until after World War II. Many of our purchases today are wants and not needs. Stop and think: Is that new car a want or a need?

The Treadle Sewing Machine

$\mathcal{T}$he treadle sewing machine was a necessary item in the early homes, as yard goods were purchased for most of our needs. If a woman wasn't a good seamstress, she could barter with a neighbor to get her clothes made. My mother was a dressmaker and made clothes for many people.

There were very few store-bought clothes in the 1930s and '40s and they usually came from Burpee's or Benedict's stores or the Montgomery Ward catalog. All their housedresses were alike, so if you wanted something different than your neighbor, you had to purchase yard goods and make your own. Patterns were usually homemade and cut out in the shape of a dress, much as a child would make doll clothes, with a belt at the waistline.

Nearly every woman could sew well enough to make her own patchwork quilts, or have a neighbor help her. Everyone used roller towels in their kitchen. They purchased toweling by the yard and made their towels the length they desired. These were a rough linen or huck towel, not like our hand towels of the 1990s. Nearly everyone could use the sewing machine to make roller towels and sausage bags and pot holders.

Everything was patched and even the patches were patched. Socks were darned by hand and every home had a wooden darning egg to put in the sock to hold it firm for darning.

The big project was bed sheets, and nearly every woman could sew well enough to supply the family with bed linens. We bought five yards of unbleached muslin for each sheet. This five-yard piece was cut into two two-and-a-half-yard pieces and sewn together the long way with the selvage on the two outside edges. Then the top and bottom were hemmed. We now had a new sheet with a hem up the center. Material only came thirty-six inches wide at that time.

The old sheets that were worn thin in the center were torn at the center seam and the two outside selvage edges sewn together on the treadle sewing machine. Sometimes these sheets were used to make draw sheets or smaller sheets for single beds or cribs. A draw sheet was a sheet used over the bottom sheet across the bed where the lower body lay to keep the bottom sheet clean in case of accidents. The smaller pieces of the worn sheet were used to make pillow cases and handkerchiefs.

Nothing went to waste at our house, and the old Wilcox and Gibbs sewing machine was always ready to go. My mother used the same old treadle sewing machine for more than sixty years and would never get the new electric ones.

First Day of Fishing Season

*A*fter a long winter, the first day of fishing was the first sign of spring. This was usually around the beginning of April. The snow was still on the banks of the brook and the water was high and ice cold. But nothing could take away the thrill of the first day of fishing.

My first pole was just a stick—I think it was dogwood or bamboo—with about ten feet of line tied on the end. A hook was attached to the end of the line with a sinker about ten inches up the line from the hook. We had never heard of special spinning or fly reels or rods. My father used pieces of an old rod that he had put together and an old hand reel.

My father's birthday was April 25. In about 1943 I bought him a nice extension pole for one dollar from Burpee's Store. I inherited his old pole and my brother got my old cane pole. I later purchased my first extension pole from Burpee's Store.

After digging worms and checking in the canvas fishing bag for extra hooks and sinkers and a ruler, I was ready to get an early start up Wells Hill to Fiddler's Elbow to fish the brook down. I usually had my limit of ten seven-inch trout by the time I reached a spot behind our house. I caught as many fish with my old stick pole as I ever caught when I was older and had a special pole and reel.

The trees along the brook have grown so thick that it is impossible to get down through there now. It would even be impossible to walk the center of the brook, but I have been tempted to try it.

I always looked forward to the first day of fishing season and my catch of fresh fish. Even worms are nearly impossible to find now, but back then I never had any trouble filling a Prince Albert tobacco can with worms for the first day of fishing season.

Spring Plowing

*A*bout the middle of May my father would say, "Spring is coming and the ground will soon be warm enough to plant the garden." His first concern was getting someone with horses and a plow and disc harrow to get the ground ready.

Before they came to plow my father covered the ground with well-rotted cow manure. This was a slow process as he had to haul it from the barnyard to the fields with a wheelbarrow.

Rolland Bronson plowed our garden for several years, but about 1945 he got a steady job and couldn't do it anymore. His brother John had just returned from the service and he took over our spring plowing. This was an all-day job as we planted about three acres. My mother always planned a large special meal, since a man coming to plow meant company for dinner.

They plowed in the forenoon and were ready to harrow in the afternoon. The disc harrows smoothed the ground and broke up the clods. I loved to follow the plow and pick up the fish worms. It was a lot easier than digging for them with a shovel. By noon I had lots of worms and was ready to go fishing.

John Bronson was the last man hired to plow our garden. After that we got our own horse and plow, and I no longer got to pick up the fish worms as I had to lead the horse while my father managed the plow. Since we didn't have harrows, we had to rake the area with a metal rake before it could be planted.

Then we were ready to get the marker to mark the length and width of the rows. This marker was a homemade wood frame measured to the exact width of the row and pulled the length of the garden. Sometimes the same one was used to pull across the width of the garden and sometimes we used one with different spacing, depending on what was being planted. Then we were ready to dig the holes at the spots where the vertical and horizontal lines met.

With a hoe we dug a hole about four inches deep and dropped in the seeds. We never bought any seeds as everyone saved and dried their own from previous years. We used different amounts for different crops. For example, corn had three kernels in a hill—one to grow, one to rot, and one for the crow.

Housecleaning Before Vacuum Cleaners

As soon as we had a couple of nice days in the spring all the women started to talk about housecleaning. They had spent the winter planning which rooms they would paper. They had already ordered the paper from the Penn Wallpaper Company book. I could never understand why the price said per single roll but you could only buy double rolls. So the price was double what the book said. It is sold the same way today. Much like pricing butter by the half pound but you have to buy a pound.

As everyone had woodstoves, everything in the house was smoked and dirty. My father would take the miles of stovepipe down and clean it before the housecleaning could start. The living room stove would be carried to the woodshed for the summer.

We started by hauling everything out of the closets. We scrubbed down the walls, woodwork, and floors. Everything was washed or aired before being put back. Next came the bedrooms—scrubbing everything, usually papering or painting the ceilings, painting the woodwork, then papering the walls. The curtains were soaked in several waters, then washed, rinsed, and starched and put on curtain frames to dry.

After our pricked fingers were forgotten and the mattress wiped off and aired and the coiled springs cleaned with a cloth on a stick, windows were washed with kerosene and water to make them shine. The floors were scrubbed and the cracks were dug clean with a knife. We had no vacuum cleaners to suck dirt from cracks and corners. We had to get down on our knees and dig them clean where a mop or broom or rag wouldn't reach. I was always sent to Lulu Nichols to buy Uka, a cleaning powder, and a pink substance to clean the wallpaper in the rooms that were not being papered.

We used the kitchen range for heating the water for cleaning. Blankets and quilts could only be washed in May or September as that was the best time for drying in a breeze. The living room, kitchen, pantry, and cellarway were done much the same way. The wood furniture was scrubbed, sanded, and varnished to a shine. The linoleum was scrubbed and varnished. The living room was usually papered and painted every year or two and everyone had to have scenery paper.

The pantry and cellarway were done much the same way except we had to put on new shelf paper and edging. Like the other rooms, everything had to be cleaned or aired so that meant washing every dish. That was my job, in the pantry. Next came the kitchen and a new piece of shelf paper and edging for the clock shelf. We always had a new oilcloth tablecloth for the big round kitchen table. The good parts of the old cloth were used to replace the ones by the pitcher pump and on the wall behind the sink. The rest of the old tablecloth was used around the separator and the top of the ice box.

Once June arrived all the women got involved in the garden and the strawberry crop. The subject of conversation during the strawberry season was, "Have you got your housecleaning done?" I think I would be insulted or burst out laughing if someone asked me that today. But that was the usual conversation starter for women in the 1930s, just as the men would ask, "Have you planted your 'taters?" or "Have you finished your haying?" or, in the fall, "Have you dug your 'taters?"

After a summer of canning and gathering apples, nuts, and produce from the garden, canning chickens, butchering the pigs and beef, it was time to do the fall housecleaning. The fall cleaning was much the same as in the spring but to a lesser degree with no papering or painting. The living room stove had to be brought back in and the miles of pipe installed before hunting season, as my father always went hunting for wild game and that meant preserving the venison, usually in mincemeat for pies.

Then we'd stuff rags into all the cracks with a silver knife and look forward to winter and Christmas.

Haying in the 1930s

*H*aying was a family project. My father would get up early and cut the hay with a scythe before he went to work. As soon as I got home from school, work, or berry picking, it was my job to rake the hay into windrows. A windrow was just a long row of hay across the field. Then the windrows were put into stacks.

After an early evening snack we all went out to carry the hay to the barn. My father, mother, and I each had a long rope that we placed on the ground in a circle. We put all the hay we could carry on the rope and brought the ends through. We placed the load on our backs and held the two loose ends of the rope over our shoulders with our hands. We carried the hay from 100 to 500 feet to the barn.

About 1945 my mother's brother gave us a horse, and we already had a wagon and a one-horse plow. The horse made our work much easier as we could load the hay on the wagon. I got to ride the wagon to the barn on top of the hay. We also could now plow our own gardens, and my job was to lead the horse for plowing.

We worked from daylight to dark every day of the year. No one ever had problems sleeping at our house. We did our homework at night by lamplight after a hard day. Is it any wonder children often went to school without their homework finished or not making any sense? I don't think the teachers knew how people from out of town lived.

World War II

$\mathscr{I}$ had just turned eleven years old when the Japanese attacked Pearl Harbor on December 7, 1941. I was in sixth grade at the Lewis Center School. We lived a very sheltered, isolated life so I wasn't really aware of what the war was all about. A neighbor who lived several miles away drove over to tell us about the Japanese attack. We hadn't heard as we hadn't had the radio on.

I knew that when the air raid warning came my father went to the Lewis Town Hall and rang the bell for the blackout. Everyone had to turn their lights out until the all-clear bells were rung. I remember it as a scary ordeal. My father also watched for airplanes.

People left this area to go to Connecticut for defense work and men went into the service. Then there was more work for the people left in the area and wages were going up.

I remember Mrs. Egglefield, one of the teachers, coming into our classroom and telling us that Bob Egglefield and Bill James had been killed in action. I also remember Harold Lamb being killed and feeling bad for the family. His death was at the end of the war.

During the war we were unable to buy a lot of things—film, nylons, tires, cars, and meat were some of the things nearly impossible to get. Sugar and canned goods required ration stamps. The shortage of sugar was a hardship on my family as my mother canned and baked a lot of pies and cakes as well as making berry and apple and rhubarb sauce.

People who didn't do their own canning really didn't get enough canned vegetables and so on, especially men living alone. I remember one older man who had nothing to eat as he had used up his canned good stamps, and he traded sugar stamps with my mother. She never used her canned good stamps and always ran out of sugar, so this helped both parties.

By 1943 I was earning a little money picking berries to sell and I always bought defense stamps and had two or three bonds by the end of the war. The stamps cost 25 cents each and it cost $18.75 to buy a $25 bond.

I'm sure an eleven-year-old today would be much more aware of what was going on now that they have radio, television, and newspapers. All we had then was a radio that we could only have on for a very few minutes a day.

Getting Home

On the way to our house on Wells Hill we had to walk by an abandoned house and barn that were close to the road. Grover Cornwright, the man who owned the property, loved animals and used the barn and land as a home for a variety of creatures. There were sheep, cattle, a donkey, geese, and ponies as well as doves and pigeons. During World War II a man from town went in the service and his pet sheep also ended up at the farm.

One day my mother, brother, and I were going to my grandmother's. My brother rode the bicycle down the hill to her house and I went in the car with my mother. When it was time to go home, my brother talked me into taking the bicycle back for him.

I rode a short distance and then pushed the bike up the hill. Once I got to the old house I was on level ground and could ride again. The barn was about fifty feet past the house and the big sheep was in the barnyard. Out he came and ran up the road ahead of me. All of a sudden he turned to come toward me with his head down. I knew I was in trouble, so I jumped off the bicycle and put it between me and the sheep.

How he did bunt that bike! When he got tired of bunting he would turn and run up the road to get a better start to bunt me again. He did this many times until I was in sight of our house and I could scream for my mother to come with the car to get me. When she got there the sheep was having too much fun to let me in the car. My mother had to drive into the ditch, and I threw the bike as my brother opened the car door. The sheep even had fun bunting the car.

My mother drove to town and got Grover to come and take care of the sheep. When Grover got there he got out of the car and the sheep came up to him. He put his hand on the sheep's head and said, "What do you think you are doing?

Come along." It was as if the terrifying experience had never taken place and that sheep made me look foolish.

The sheep soon came up missing and I could go to town again. I found out that the sheep had been raised on a bottle in a house full of boys who played rough with him. We had never had a sheep and I was terrified when he came for me. I didn't realize all he wanted was to play rough.

I've often wondered if my brother knew what the sheep would do and decided to play another joke on his sister. Getting home that day was an experience I have never forgotten, but I have had many laughs over that sheep.

Thirteen Years Old in 1943

The year was 1943 and World War II had been going for nearly two years. Money was more abundant but everyone still had to work very hard for everything.

I was going into seventh grade in September, just as I turned thirteen years old. This was a big event, since I would be leaving Lewis and moving into the Elizabethtown school, and I needed new clothes. Getting the money was no problem as wild berries were abundant and people had money to buy them.

First came the wild strawberries, which had to be picked and hulled. These sold for fifty cents a quart. Once the strawberries were gone we went to raspberries, then blackberries, and last came the blueberries. They all sold for twenty-five cents a quart. I was able to earn 100 dollars from June to September picking berries, which allowed me to buy several dresses, a winter coat, and other articles of clothing, as well as keeping me in spending money all winter. I could only have one pair of shoes, though, as shoes were rationed and people in the cold North Country needed boots and warm footwear. So nothing fancy could be purchased during the war.

I sent an order to Montgomery Ward for a red-and-white striped, drop-waist dress for one dollar. My best dress cost two dollars. It had a sailor-type collar and was the latest style. It was navy blue with white trim. My winter coat was a practical maroon wool tweed. I was very proud to show off my clothes closet under the chimney that contained my special new clothes.

Fifty years later, I remember that I worked very hard to earn that money but no one was ever happier or more proud of their accomplishments than I was in 1943. A thirteen-year-old would never work that hard for a new wardrobe and spending money these days. And we don't have the berries today for anyone to pick. Trees have crowded out the berries and houses now occupy the fields that were vacant in 1943.

School Days

In 1943 I was ready to leave the Lewis Center School and go into seventh grade. I had fears worse than any I'd ever had before.

Here I was having to go the four miles to Elizabethtown to school, a town I had only been to a couple of times before in my lifetime. Only four other students that I knew were going. I had to leave behind all the others from the small Lewis school where everyone played together and was treated equally. I found myself in a classroom with twenty-seven students, all strangers, and teachers I had never seen before. I was terrified.

One of my first experiences in seventh grade was when the teacher went from one classroom to another and we were left alone for about five minutes. The girl behind me put her feet under my chair and pulled it, taking me by surprise and dumping me on the floor.

Just then our teacher, Mrs. Egglefield, came through the door and punished me for being out of my seat. I tried to explain what had happened but she called me a baby and said she only knew what she saw. This incident hurt me physically and mentally and from that day on I hated school and could never adjust.

The teachers never went into the restroom during "basement" period. (For some reason, we called the bathroom the "basement" even though it was on the same floor.) It was a horror chamber for anyone who had been taught privacy.

The girls from Elizabethtown stuck together and never got caught for any of their escapades. Many of the students who came from the more isolated areas were not ready to cope with society due to their sheltered lives. My family was still living on Wells Hill with no electricity, telephone, or indoor plumbing. Cars were very scarce and there was no money for gasoline. Unless you lived in Elizabethtown, it was impossible to participate in many school activities.

We still had to wear long brown stockings and lots of weird heavy clothing. I had two long bus waits in the cold just to get to school in Elizabethtown. Every morning I was cold and sick to my stomach.

When I went on to high school the war had ended and everything had advanced financially and socially, so it wasn't such a scary place. But because I had a bad start, I never liked school again. After I was fifty years old I attended and graduated from North Country Community College and really enjoyed that learning experience.

Is Bigger Better?

$\mathcal{T}$he end of the war brought a lot of changes into everyone's lives. The boys were coming home and many with new brides. Some only stayed for a short time while others made this area their home. The sawmills were going full blast and there was work for many people for the first time in their lives.

Many changes were taking place in our family and my life. For the first time in my lifetime my father was able to find full-time work and our lives were beginning to be easier and we didn't have to work as hard on our few acres.

In 1946, when I was sixteen years old and my brother was eleven, my parents had the opportunity to buy a big house in town. The only home I had ever known was the log house on Wells Hill. I couldn't see anything wrong with that four-room cabin with its low ceilings and pitcher pump in the kitchen. The "necessary" building (our name for the outhouse) was out in the cold beyond the woodshed and we took baths in the kitchen or carried water upstairs to our bedrooms.

My mother had decided she was going to live in town and have modern conveniences. So in October of 1946 we moved into the big five-bedroom house. Well, we nearly froze to death the first winter in that big house in the center of Lewis. We were used to the small, cozy, warm log house and had no idea that a big house would be so cold and drafty.

My father kept making improvements and finally installed insulation to make the house comfortable. The "necessary" building was outside for the first year, then we had a modern bathroom. We had electricity and our own bedrooms, spare rooms, an electric flatiron, a toaster, and running water. We also had hot water after the first year.

My father didn't give up his animals and the farm life when we moved, even though this house only had a couple of acres. I never went to the barn or helped with the barn chores once we moved. When we lived on Wells Hill I used to go to the barn

Views of Lewis, Late '20s or early '30s

every night to help with the milking, and feed the cats and the calf and pigs. I could never go into the barn at the new house, though. This place was never really home to me.

We had a cat that wouldn't move with us. No matter how many times we transported her to her new home, she wouldn't stay. My brother would go back to Wells Hill every day and bring her down, but she would go right back to her old home. After the weather got real cold she moved down the road to a neighbor's barn and raised a family.

I always felt like the cat, that my home was on the hill in the little log house with all the hard work and struggle for survival. Many years after we left, the house burned, but every detail of the house and the farm is clear in my memories.

My first sixteen years of life in the small house left happy memories, and I find it hard to remember the hardships we took for granted. Everyone else had few conveniences and, as far as I was concerned, I really didn't miss them.

Apparently my mother knew there was an easier way to live and was determined to try for a better life. But my father and I were ready to move back on the hill anytime, even though there was no electricity or telephone lines. If we mentioned this, my mother always put her foot down, saying, "You know we are a lot better off here close to town and all the conveniences."

Never Say Quit

$\mathscr{I}$n 1980, when I turned fifty years old, I decided to take a course in Small Business Management to learn some skills. I had been out of school for over thirty years and the world had changed so much that I felt incompetent to compete with our increased home bookkeeping. Balancing our budget and our checkbook was much more complex than in 1949.

After completing the one course, I knew I needed more education to cope with the other areas where I lacked skills. I soon enrolled at North Country Community College as a full-time student while holding down a full-time job. After my day at work I couldn't be tired as I had to be in class five evenings a week from six to nine o'clock.

Several of the classes were held in Ticonderoga, Crown Point, or Saranac Lake. This was a long drive at night in all kinds of weather. All spare time had to be spent studying or researching materials for term papers. I often put material for tests on tape and played it after I went to bed at night or while traveling to classes. As a result of my hard work, I made the dean's list several times.

Many times I felt the urge to quit and would question: "What does this degree mean to me at my age? Why am I working every minute of my life to get my degree?"

When I had one more semester left to earn an Associate's Degree, the college changed its course of study. Several of the classes I had taken would no longer count in my program. This meant about a year and a half more of full-time study if I wanted to graduate.

It had been a long, hard, physical, mental, and financial struggle to get as far as I had. But my desire to get my degree won over all my negative feelings and, at fifty four years of age, I received my Associate's Degree—a two-year program that took me four years.

Learning is an ongoing process and if we are open to education there are always new things to learn. Never say quit! There are many ways to learn and I still do a lot of reading and studying and taking classes.

My Life Today

In August of 1991 I left my job as program director at a senior center. In December I received a telephone call from a state park in Florida where I had applied as a volunteer. They wanted me as soon as my husband, John, and I could get there. Four days later we were in Sebring, Florida, ready to go to work.

Highlands Hammock is a beautiful park with lots of deer and other wild animals as well as lovely orange groves. We fell in love with the area as well as the people and the work. I worked at this busy park for three winters; my job was toll collector at the ranger station. I also worked at the ranger station in the Little Manatee River State Recreational Area, and as campground host at Hillsborough River State Park. So far I have more than 1,200 volunteer hours at state parks.

We always return to Lewis in the spring and stay until late fall. For the past three summers I have been a volunteer at the Essex County Historical Society doing geneology research. I have been interested in geneology all my life and I finally have time to do what I want to do. I am also interested in local history and have filled many scrapbooks and files. I have nearly completed the history of the many district schools in the Town of Lewis from 1814 to 1988. I am also putting together a history of the Town.

Retirement has not been a time of leisure but a time to do everything I want to do. The family, garden, canning, research, and volunteer work keep every day full. I make rugs, knit, crochet, and try different crafts. I even find time to read a book once in awhile.

My husband is very active walking, bike riding, gardening, and keeping the yard and garden presentable. We have been married thirty-three years.

Sonja Aubin

$\mathcal{I}$ was born in April, 1936, to Hattie J. Bronson and Floyd W. Cassavaugh. I was the third child in a family of seven children; three of my brothers are now deceased. I spent all my youth and adolescence in the dwelling my father and grandfather built on what is now the Moss Road in Stowersville, a small settlement just east of the Northway in the Town of Lewis.

I married Claude W. Aubin in 1955 and had five children. My first child passed away at the age of eight months. I have lived on Water Street in Elizabethtown for about thirty-five years. Most of my working life was spent at a typewriter as a secretary. I've enjoyed sewing, crafts, oil painting, and writing.

Elementary Education

I started school in a one-room schoolhouse. It was less than a mile from my house on what is now the Moss Road in Stowersville, across the Northway from Lewis. Five grades were housed in this tiny little school, but there were no more than ten students in a class.

The year was 1942 and I was six years old. I had an older brother, an older sister, and several cousins in the school with me. I already knew just about everyone else who attended.

From the very beginning I believe our teacher instilled a sense of fear in all of us. It may have been the method she used to control such a large number of children who came from such big families and who were of such different ages. The older boys could be very unruly and the younger children were too bashful and shy. The teacher was very tough except when holidays began to roll around and then she softened up a bit.

In this one-room schoolhouse every class was taught separately. That meant that sometimes the older children would judge the younger ones as not moving ahead as fast as they should. Then the older children would report this back to the parents. Occasionally the younger ones would tattle on the older ones for misbehaving.

This situation sometimes caused tension and dissension among the parents and the brothers and sisters. It could lead to very negative reactions and a great deal of unnecessary discipline. There was hardly any rapport between parents and teacher, except when the report cards went home to be signed. The only other reports that went to our homes were usually negative ones.

Despite all these problems, we did learn to read, write, and do arithmetic. A great part of the day was spent reading, although the books were always shared. Each student was expected to go to the front of the class to recite their lessons.

The worst times were when we didn't know the words. We were disciplined by the hit of a ruler or the whack of a teacher's hand.

I often thought that discipline must have been the number one priority for both teachers and parents. I felt the children were being punished because of the parents' feelings of frustration over their own shortcomings or lack of educational skills. This was an area where an education in parenting skills would have benefited the adults as well as the children.

I don't believe any of us realized that we might be in a category called poverty-stricken, but today we could be considered so. We probably could have been thought of as poverty-stricken, deprived, maladjusted, unsociable, overly shy, and sometimes aggressive and much more. There was no one in our one-room schoohouse to put any labels on us except the teacher and our own classmates.

This schoolhouse had no running water, no electricity, no telephone, and no central heating. The water was either carried in by the teacher or fetched by the students from down a long hill. It was brought up to the school in a five-gallon, galvanized pail that usually came back only half full because the rest spilled out along the difficult trek up the hill.

The water came from an underground spring and ran into a wooden barrel. It always tasted fresh and cool and I'm sure it was never tested to see if it was fit to drink. Sanitation didn't seem to enter into it. We all drank from the same dipper and then it was replaced on a shelf.

There was a woodstove at the back of the schoolroom that was supposed to keep us warm. But during the long winter days there was never a nice, even heat. We were always too hot or too cold. Mostly I recall cold hands and cold feet. The teacher and the older boys were responsible for keeping this old stove going. No one ever objected to the task of filling the stove with wood.

On dark days there was very little light in the schoolhouse. Kerosene lanterns or lamps were used when the winter days were overcast. Electricity didn't come to our area until I was about 14 years old.

We also didn't have telephones until I was a teenager, so there was no communication during the day between teacher and parents or parents and children. If someone was sick, the teacher took care of it in the best way she saw fit. Colds, measles, whooping cough, mumps, head lice, and just plain homesickness could be problems for the teacher, as well as for parents who had to contend with the illness.

Children admitting they were sick could be an ordeal. Many times the teacher or the parents didn't know exactly how to handle the illness and they became frustrated. A doctor could not be called on the spot and he also had to come many miles. There was often no transportation to take a child to the doctor. Stomach bugs, influenza, and pneumonia were strictly a parent's problem. Bed rest and plenty of liquids usually did the trick.

There was no cafeteria, of course. Usually the mothers made a small lunch of biscuits or home-baked bread. Some students didn't bring a lunch at all. This meant that they asked for part of someone else's or they had to endure hunger for the rest of the day. A nutritious lunch was not a high priority for some families.

Chemical toilets, one for the boys and one for the girls, were at each side of the entrance. When I started school I don't believe we had access to toilet paper. I think we might have used old catalogs. There were shelves on each side of the entrance for bagged lunches. Again, the idea of sanitation did not exist, since we stored our lunches so close to the toilets.

There were also hooks for coats or sweaters, but some children did not have a coat or sweater to hang on the hooks. The fact was that some families were too poor to buy them one or they didn't have the sewing skills to make them one. Money to buy coats might not have been in the budget because there were very few jobs and few people had job skills.

No one got a newspaper to help students keep up with world events or daily happenings in the vicinity or the outside world.

Most news consisted only of what was going on around us or within our family circles. This lack of information caused a great deal of narrow-mindedness in children and adults.

Some families were extremely poor. Some children were so poor that they had no shoes and could only go to school in the fall and spring. To be poor could be very devastating for a child. They were ridiculed by other children and by their own parents. The children carried the "sin" of being born and putting such a burden on their parents. They were ostracized at home and at school. They felt responsible for their own deprived state.

Alcoholism in some families produced very unhappy children. It was usually the fathers who drank. I think it was because they couldn't cope with the fact that there was no work in the area and they lost their feeling of self-worth.

Those people who lived on farms were much more fortunate than those who didn't. On a farm the whole family worked together to survive. Milking, feeding the animals, butchering, and gardening were everybody's work. The meat supply came from the chickens, pigs, and cows. There was plenty of milk to drink, although it wasn't pasteurized. Pork, beef, and eggs supplied the necessary proteins for good health.

Gardening was another family project. Vegetables, such as potatoes, green beans, tomatoes, pumpkins, squash, cucumbers, lettuce, and radishes were grown. Corn was an important vegetable because it also could be fed to the animals. Apple trees and berries grew in the area.

We endured in spite of the conditions. My older brother took fifth and sixth grades together and excelled all through school. My older sister continued her education at Albany Business College and became a secretary. Most of the children who grew up in this location and attended this one-room schoolhouse have done well in spite of the odds and the underprivileged conditions.

My Mother's Life

𝒯here were many frustrating times for my mother when she was raising her family. Some may have been more trivial than others, but her complaints were real and legitimate. In spite of her best efforts, she was often defeated by her circumstances.

Some of those circumstances included the task of starting the fire in the early morning to prepare breakfast for several hungry mouths. If she hadn't had time the day before to gather all the materials for the fire, she often hunted around for comic book pages (they arrived at our house via her cousin who worked in a factory in Connecticut). Other fire starters were cardboard boxes or pages from the *Grit* newspaper.

After she folded and crumpled the pages, she laid them on the grates of the big kitchen cookstove. On top she put kindling wood that very often was damp. She added larger sticks of wood with a little kerosene sprinkled over the top.

All of this effort took time and sometimes proved fruitless because the fire wouldn't burn. We could often hear her complaining about the soggy wood and bad weather conditions and the fact that the chimney might need cleaning again so the fire would burn better.

Getting the fire to start sometimes took an hour or so, which meant rising early if breakfast was going to be on the table for those going to school or work. But we always ended up with a hearty breakfast of fried eggs, potatoes, and pancakes, or oatmeal and toasted homemade bread.

My mother had other hard tasks as well. Carrying the water must have been the most difficult. The spring was a long way from our house. We had to cross the main road to reach it. We walked across a long meadow that looked like a hayfield and then down a long hill. At the bottom was the spring. I recall my mother using a yoke to carry two pails of water.

The spring often froze over in the winter. Chopping the ice away to get a pail of drinking water was tedious and exhausting. Trudging through heavy snow up a long hill several times a day wore her out as well. She often complained of shoulder and back pain.

Canning fruits and vegetables went on all summer. She spent long hours over the hot woodstove. In the fall and winter it was always a disappointment to her when she went to the cellar to get a jar of string beans or peaches and it had not sealed tight and was spoiled. Sometimes she felt as though her labors were in vain. Because we were children we weren't as sympathetic with her disappointments as we might have been.

Even though my mother seemed to have a time clock inside her that helped her judge when she had to complete all the tasks that fell upon her, she was often interrupted by a neighbor who wanted her to wash and curl her hair, a child's sick-

My mother and father, Hattie and Floyd
Cassavaugh

ness, or her close relatives who occasionally called her to their bedside during sickness or childbirth. At those times she had to work extra hard to complete all the home tasks that would keep her family unit running smoothly while taxing herself with other people's problems.

All in all, even though my mother was efficient, hard-working, and focussed on her family, there were times that she would have welcomed a vacation away from her laborious lifestyle. Those relaxing times didn't come until much later after her last child left home. It was only then that she and my dad bought a motor home and traveled to Louisiana, Florida, and elsewhere.

Running Water at Our House

 long with other men from our area, my father had learned to use a "witch stick" to hunt for water. It was believed that a branch from a willow or apple tree would work the best. The branch was shaped like a V with a long handle in the front. My father held the ends of the V in each hand. As he walked over a slight ravine on our back property and along a flat area, he discovered water. The witch stick had turned downward toward the ground. It was a sign that water ran underneath the surface of the earth.

At that location my father drove down a well point. This was a pipe with a string running through it and a weight and knot at the end. When the weight came up wet, it was a sure sign that water was there. After my father's discovery, he hooked a pump to the pipe and checked to see how many gallons of water could be pumped up. He then laid more pipe up to our house and installed a hand pump in our kitchen. By priming the pump with dippers of water, we could move the handle up and down and the water would be forced from the well.

My father's efforts paid off. We all took turns pumping water. Wash and bath days now came more frequently and the dread of carrying the heavy water pails was over.

Even more progress was to come soon. Electricity, "man's most useful servant," was coming to our area. Our house was wired and a new electric water pump was installed. My father built a new bathroom with a lavatory, bathtub, and toilet and piped water to it. He hooked up a new sink in the corner of the kitchen. A new washing machine was purchased that required less effort. We could now have a vacuum cleaner to make our housework easier. In the evening there was more leisure time for playing games and better lighting for doing our homework.

All of these great things came to us between 1946 and 1948. Due to my father's firm belief in progress, life improved with much, much less drudgery.

The Chicks Have Come

In the 1930s, '40s, and '50s around our area in Stowersville, nearly everyone raised chickens for the eggs and meat they provided. It was an exciting time for the children in our family when the mailman pulled up to our Rural Free Delivery mailbox and honked the horn. We knew a package had arrived, although it was only once a year—in the early spring—when a package came that peeped.

A couple of sturdy, flat cardboard boxes with round holes cut in the top were passed over to us children to carry to the house. When we took off the top the chickens were all matted together with their beaks pointed up in a peeping mass. Sometimes a few of them had died.

Mom and Dad always checked the order form to see if the right number of chicks had arrived. They usually ordered fifty or sixty. We were told not to handle the little chicks too much or they might die.

A brooder was then set up inside a warm place in the house with plenty of chicken feed and water. The brooder had a high, cone-shaped metal top with a light bulb in the inside and a tray around the bottom to hold the grain. Each day everyone checked to see if the chicks were well. Occasionally some died and had to be removed, which always made me feel bad.

We were all fascinated with the chicks' rapid growth. After seven or eight weeks they were ready for a bigger home. When the weather was warmer, the chickens were carried to a fenced-in area below our backyard. There was a building there with high beams where the chickens could roost. The feeding troughs were handmade and filled with corn and grain. There were watering troughs also. Hay was arranged for the nests, and after about six months we were able to start gathering the warm eggs. We always had one rooster and he was our alarm clock. He crowed "cock-a-doodle-doo" until we were all awake and ready to go to school.

After about a year the hens' egg production decreased. Then they were ready for the chopping block. We'd chase the chicken around the yard, catch it, and hand it to my mother. She'd grab it by the legs, put its neck on the block, and chop its head off with an axe. Sometimes she'd miss and get only half of the head. We'd all scream as the head came off. The chicken could run quite a ways with no head.

Their feathers were picked, pinfeathers singed over a flame, and the innards removed. Then they were cooked as fricassee chicken or in other good recipes.

The soft, yellow, peeping feathered friends that were delivered directly to our mailbox and grew into adulthood were a much-needed source of our food supply. We were rewarded generously by their existence in our backyard.

My Grandmothers

As a child, I spent a great deal of time with both of my grand-mothers. Now that I'm an adult, I have very fond memories of them. Their maiden names were Eliza Tubbs and Nora Mac-Dougal. They were born before the first car was invented, and neither of them ever learned to drive one.

Eliza was born in 1881 and lived seventy-four years. Nora was born in 1891 and lived seventy-two years. As far back as I can remember, they lived directly across the Bouquet River from one another in Stowersville. Until recently I never appreciated the hardships they had to endure during their lifetimes.

Both grandmothers were married at a very young age. My grandmother Eliza was married for the first time at age four-teen and Nora was married at fifteen. They both would eventually marry for a second time.

One interesting story that Eliza's youngest son, John, re-layed to me was about Eliza's first husband and the little girl who was born to that union. Shortly after her young marriage, Eliza discovered her husband was somewhat of a ladies' man, and the marriage soon disintegrated. He finally left her, but one day he appeared again when their little four-year-old daughter was playing in the front yard. He abducted little Flossie.

Although Eliza witnessed her child being taken away by force, she had no quick means of travel or assistance to rescue her little girl. Afterwards, she was unable to find her.

Soon after the child was kidnapped, Eliza went to live with her sister in a small settlement outside of Elizabethtown called Scrabble Hollow. While living there, she was employed at the Essex County Jail in the kitchen area. In the meantime, she met a man named Warren Bronson.

Still longing for her lost child, who by then had been missing for two years, and with the suspicion that her husband had taken the girl to Vermont, Eliza and Warren hitched a horse to a cutter and crossed frozen Lake Champlain on a dangerous journey to locate her. I was told there was about six inches of water over the surface of the ice, so I would assume spring was coming or it was a warming spell.

Luckily, her suspicions and the location she suspected her daughter to be at were exactly right. She was happily reunited with her six-year-old daughter who was very badly in need of better care. Thankfully, her first husband never bothered her again and she was divorced and married to Warren and they had five more children.

My grandmother Nora also had hardships to bear. She had married a man from Canada and he worked in the logging camps throughout the Adirondacks. His work was dangerous and he was exposed to all of the elements, but they managed to raise five children. At age forty two, he succumbed to the dreaded disease cancer. Nora, too, would eventually marry again and raise one more child.

Both grandmothers came from very large families—Eliza from a family of eleven children and Nora from a family of nine. They both had a limited amount of formal education. Eliza had gone as far as the fourth grade in a small district school, and Nora had also been deprived of higher educational opportunities. But the lack of schooling did not prevent them from reading a good recipe or a small weekly newspaper that was delivered to their homes.

Both grandmothers knew the art of serving their children and grandchildren a nutritional and balanced meal. It was always a pleasure to sit at their tables eating homemade bread with freshly churned butter, warm cottage cheese, and home-grown vegetables. The protein portion of the meal came from the chickens, hogs, and cows that they helped care for until slaughtering time.

Together, the grandmothers often hitched up the horses and went to the fields and woods to pick wild blackberries, strawberries, and blueberries. I also remember long lines of sliced apples hanging to dry on strings close to the ceiling. The apples would later be soaked and used for delicious pies.

These self-sufficient women also made their own pillows and mattresses from oat straw covered with ticking that they bought at the local store. Unfortunately, these mattresses flattened out in a couple of months and the covering had to be filled again. They saved chicken, geese, and duck feathers for pillows, and I definitely remember sleeping on a feather mattress at my grandmother Nora's home. I'll always remember a sinking-down, soft, secure feeling. It was like sleeping on a soft cloud.

I often wondered what these women's young lives were like. My uncle related this story to me: My grandmother Eliza had no shoes as a very young child. She would often run to the barn in the snow, gather the eggs, warm her feet in the hay, and run back to the log cabin as fast as she could. Since the

Log drive on the Boquet, circa 1908

eggs were rationed for family use, she was not allowed to eat them herself. The reason given was that the eggs must be saved to sell for the money that was so badly needed for other things.

One day while her mother was out, Eliza's desire for an egg was just too overwhelming. So she cooked one for herself and one for each of her two sisters as well. She swore her sisters to secrecy, but soon afterward her littlest sister, Idy, couldn't resist telling their mother and Eliza was reprimanded.

By March of that year, Eliza's father had sold enough eggs and handwoven bushel and pack baskets he'd made from the black ash tree to buy her a new pair of shoes. But before then, when she complained about her cold trips to the barn, barefooted, Eliza's father simply stated, "God's leather ought to withstand God's weather."

Nora's skills in speedily harnessing a horse must have come from her early childhood. I often stood in awe as she harnessed her horses. She could throw the harness over the horse's back, hook all the rings in place, and put on the bit, bridle, and blinders faster than anyone I ever knew. She would then climb aboard her buggy, crack the whip, and off she would go at a trot to visit her nearest kinfolk.

I always assumed these grandmothers had a secret to life. They had resolved their problems, endured life's hardships, and continued to smile and have fun as long as I knew them.

Wild Strawberry Picking Time

*W*ild strawberries were plentiful in the meadows and on the hillsides across from our home by about the middle of June each year. Since my oldest sister's birthday came in June, my mother always picked the wild strawberries for a shortcake that served as a birthday cake. From then on until the season was over, we had several shortcakes.

When my brothers, sisters, and I were young we were always excited when my mother chose a day and decided the weather was sunny enough to go into the fields to pick berries. Each of us took along a container. Optimistically, we went from patch to patch. We spent a good share of the day squatting down or bending over to pick the tiny, juicy berries.

While we picked, we often got separated because we concentrated so hard on filling our containers. Finally my mother or one of the others of us would realize we had distanced ourselves from the rest and we would call back and forth until there was an answer. Then we would unite to compare how full our dishes had become and combine our fruit into a large bucket. When the decision was made to leave the field, the older children would carry the pail.

Of course that wasn't the end of our work. When we got home we all sat around the table with a pile of berries in front of each of us. Another hour or more was spent hulling them.

In the meantime, my mother stoked up the woodstove, made her usual baking powder biscuit recipe, and spread it in round pans. When it was nice and brown on the top, she removed it from the pan and cut it straight through the middle. She put real homemade butter on one half and then the berries that she had crushed and mixed with sugar. Of course, she had skimmed the cream off some milk earlier and whipped it with sugar.

As you can well imagine, we had reason to smile when we took the first bite. And every bite after that just got better.

Today the Adirondack Northway runs through the property that my family owned and the place where our strawberry patches were. The mountain in back of the meadows is gone and the strawberry fields are covered with roadway.

My First Perm

$\mathcal{I}$ believe I was about thirteen or fourteen when my mother decided that my sister and I would be happy with permed hair. While we were growing up, long braids were popular. My mother parted our hair down the front and back, gathered a length of hair on each side of our head, and wove them into two long braids. Other times she parted long strands of hair just in the very front above our foreheads and rolled it back. The rest of our long hair hung loose.

My mother's decision that we were ready for curly hair brought her, my sister, and me to Mrs. Tingley, a hairdresser in nearby Willsboro. My mother was very comfortable with the beauty parlor setting since she had been there before, but I was apprehensive about ruining my long blond hair.

I don't remember anything about the shampoo or the hair-cut. What does stick in my mind were the electric cords with curlers on the ends that hung from somewhere up above. They were put on my hair to heat it until it curled. About halfway through my perm I felt a terrible burning sensation on the back of my neck and the top of my head. It was difficult to turn my head because it was so weighted down with metal curlers. I just remember feeling very faint.

Finally, the hairdresser came to check and saw that I had two bad blisters on the back of my neck. When she removed the curlers I wasn't too happy with the way I looked. Since I had never had curly hair, it was a strange new me that I saw in the mirror. My appearance had changed drastically in just a couple of hours.

Even though I was determined to never again have another perm, I later changed my mind. It wasn't long before the Toni and Lilt home permanent kits came on the market. My mother and sisters and I experimented on each other and found out we could have good results. Over the years we all learned to follow the directions, roll the hair, apply the solutions, and wait the proper time for the curling process.

During those times, we enjoyed being able to sit in Ma's kitchen, catch up on the gossip, and come out feeling more confident and looking more debonaire.

Saturday Night Square Dancing

Square dancing was a popular pastime in our area in the 1940s and '50s. All we really had to know were the basic movements. We could learn the rest by watching the other dancers.

The American Legion had bought the Methodist Church in Lewis and had to find a way to pay their bills. They decided to have square dancing every Saturday night from 9 p.m. until 1 a.m. Many Legionnaires and their wives turned out to make it a success. A kitchen was installed where Michigan hot dogs, pickled eggs, potato chips, and other snacks were served. Usually three or four people volunteered each night to serve the crowd.

The night was complete when the crowd from Lewis arrived. The men, women, and children came in their finest garments. The men were handsome in their best ironed and creased trousers, starched shirts, and polished shoes. Their hair was slicked back with scented hair tonic.

The women also took pride in their appearance. Most often, women wore dresses or skirts and blouses. One of my favorite skirts was circular with a patchwork design. Black-and-white saddle shoes and white socks topped off the outfit. Like the grownups, the younger boys and girls looked neat and tidy. Ruffles, ribbons, and patent leather shoes were "in" for the girls, and it wasn't unusual to see the little boys wearing a tie.

While I attended the dances, the most renowned group that played for us was the Lytle Family—Hank, Beatrice, and their daughters, Anne Marie and Betty Jean. Other locals who occasionally entertained us were a husband-and-wife team, Win and Irene Gough, and Ida Cross and her son Richard from Lewis. Others were Al's Radio Gang from Tupper Lake, the Western Ramblers, and Lefty Girard and his Chuck Wagon Riders with Buddy Truax and Yodeling Audrey.

Some of the tunes we square danced to were "Buffalo Boy 'Go Round the Outside," "Oh, Susanna," "Dive for the Oyster,

*My sister Myrna is on the left, and my
brother Eugene is behind my elbow*

Baby and me

Dig for the Clam," and "Darling Nellie Gray." In between square dances the band played contemporary music of the era. Those were called round dances. We did waltzes, foxtrots, and polkas and danced to such Western music as "Candy Kisses," "Cold, Cold Heart," "Bouquet of Roses," and "Tennessee Waltz."

The people in our area anticipated the fun we would have on a Saturday night. The activity brought us together from our usual labors. As for me, the large, round globe-like light that hung on a long chain and showered the dancers with colored rays also hangs on in my mind, giving the long-forgotten dancers a look of perpetual rainbow motion.

Fences

*T*here are many types of fences to be seen around the vicinity of Elizabethtown and Lewis. They were used to mark boundaries, to keep animals in, and to protect domestic animals from wild animals. Some fences were used for beautification purposes. The fences were made of wire, stone, stumps, and wood.

To me, the most fascinating fence was a stump fence. I would assume that after a tree was cut down, a strong horse pulled the stumps out of the ground. They were then laid on top of the ground with the roots pointing upward. Along our property in Stowersville, a stump fence was used to separate my mother and father's property from Rob Cross's hayfield.

The roots of the trees went every which way, but someone had placed all the stumps in a line to create a beautiful fence. We were only allowed to cross it during haying time when my uncle cut the hay for his animals. Spotted adders and grass snakes lived in the stump fence and now and then they appeared out of their cozy home to scare us.

As you drive throughout the North Country, you will find many stone fences. Some appear along the back roads or in fields. Rocks used to build and form the sturdy stone fences vary in size, shape, and color and one could spend a whole day admiring their beauty and imagining the time and patience it took to complete such a work of art. Obviously, many, many man-hours must have gone into carrying, choosing, and placing the stones—without cement or mortar—to insure the future stability of the fence.

The most useful fence that came to our area was the electric fence, although it seemed cruel at times when the horses or cows bumped against it and were startled. We knew the sensation the animals got from the short contact with the fence because my cousins and other children in our family often dared each other to grab on to see the results. We'd get a shock that went right down to the balls of our feet. We didn't know whether to laugh or cry, but we at least found out why the animals didn't venture beyond it.

Our hogs were enclosed in a pen with a wooden fence around it on the back of our property. The hogs often rooted with their snouts and made holes under the fence. They escaped to my uncle's property and then to the fields across from our house. Our family made a merry chase through the tall grass, with the hogs squealing and grunting. We often caught hold of their short, fat bodies, but they got away and off they would go again, oink, oink, oinking, until a couple of people found the right technique and then the conquest was over. Little did the hogs know that they would soon be on our plates as pork chops, spareribs, bacon, and sausage.

Other fences that were used to keep farm animals from escaping were barbed wire and chicken wire, but sometimes the cows and horses did get through even the best constructed

Remains of a stump fence

barbed wire fence. Chickens often flew over the tops of their meshed wire fences or wild animals such as foxes, weasels, coy dogs, bobcats, or even hawks could attack the poultry population.

Today a barbed wire fence that was constructed along old property lines many, many years ago can sometimes be found growing through the bark or heart of an old tree The sturdy stump fence can be found in the most remote meadows or wooded areas. All the fences had a purpose and a character that served and protected the precious property each family called its own.

Wildflowers in Stowersville

$\mathcal{D}$uring the late spring and summer months, our family took special pleasure picking the wildflowers that grew around our house and in the meadows. We were seldom without a bouquet on our table. When the arrangement finally wilted there was usually a new one to replace it. The fact that we used just a drinking glass or a quart canning jar for a vase never reduced the pleasure we saw in the beautiful flowers.

The first sign of spring brought the May flowers. Later came buttercups, paint brushes, black-eyed Susans, daisies, honeysuckle, baby toes, mountain laurel, clover, and Queen Anne's lace. Back in the wooded area were violets, lady slippers, jack-in-the-pulpit, and trilliums (better known to us children as stink pots because they smelled so bad). Jack-in-the pulpit resembles a minister standing in a pulpit and lady slippers are shaped like a shoe.

My mother always warned us not to pick the trilliums or lady slippers because they were protected by law. The trilliums bloomed in the damp, shady woods and the petals were white, but gradually turned pink. Later on we learned that the running cedar that grew close to the ground was also protected. We had once used it to decorate our windows at Christmas time.

A fresh bouquet of flowers brightened all our days. All summer long my brothers and sisters could run through the high grass and choose the flowers we thought smelled the sweetest or looked the prettiest. We also liked to pick the lilacs that grew on the south side of the road from our house on the Moss Road. The pretty purple and white blossoms smelled especially sweet and so did the apple and cherry blossoms.

Now when the beginning of summer arrives I go to a greenhouse to choose my flower garden selections. I'm able to admire their beauty and share them with my friends. But the real pleasure was when I participated in the simple childhood activity of picking Adirondack wildflowers. It kept me and my brothers and sisters occupied for a time and often put a smile on my mother Hattie's face. Of course when we were happy, so was she.

My father on horseback, with my uncle leading

Horses

Years ago, horses were very important to the people of the Adirondacks. Nearly all of my relatives and neighbors owned at least one horse and many owned several. Mostly they were used for work, but they were also our companions. If they weren't too feisty, they would give us a pleasant ride.

Horses helped with the hard work like skidding logs, plowing gardens, and pulling hay wagons. Some were used for race-horses. They pulled sleighs in the winter and buggies in nice weather. Good horses were a prized possession and nearly everyone I knew had a barn to keep them in. When the crops were harvested, the horses' feed was taken into consideration just as much as the food for humans.

My father's brother Thomas always had a barn full of horses. He did a great deal of horse trading and raced at the Essex County Fair. Many times I saw him go around the race track in his racing cart at the Westport fairgrounds. He also had his own race track behind his house. His two sons and two daughters rode, trained, and exercised their horses there.

Our family often visited and rode Uncle Tom's horses. My cousins were always anxious to have us ride with them or show us what new tricks the horses could do. We learned how to groom them by brushing them and combing their tails and manes. We often watched while the horses' hooves were filed down and they got new shoes. We learned to bring them from the fields to the barn and give them hay, grain, and water and put them in their stalls. Very often we were warned to stay away from the frisky ones so we wouldn't get kicked.

My father's mother always kept horses. She also had a little Shetland pony we all rode to the Stowersville bridge and back to her house until we grew too big to ride it anymore. That little pony was the highlight of our visit and my grandmother took extra good care of her pet.

My grandfather Bronson kept horses, too. He used them mostly during haying season. His son, Uncle Bud, always rounded up his older children and the children from our family to help with the haying. After we had all raked the hay in piles, we loaded it on the hay wagon. The real fun began after we had a full load. With one helping the other we all climbed on top of the load and sank down in our own special place for a relaxing trip to the barn.

One summer when I was about 14, my father suggested that I help him peel pulp so we could get a few loads of logs to the pulp mill. I was the oldest child left at home. My sister worked during the summer at the Old Mill Art School in Elizabethtown and my brother was in the service.

The day started early with a breakfast of fried potatoes, eggs, and pancakes. I dressed in an old pair of my brother's army fatigues. They had long sleeves and covered me well to protect me from the biting black flies.

Horse trading in Stowersville

Old Kit was our workhorse and boarded in our next door neighbor's barn. I had learned how to bridle and harness a horse, and Old Kit also had a whippletree hooked to his harness with chains that helped him pull, or skid, logs. He was always anxious to get to work by the time the leather straps were all in place. He didn't need instructions to find the wood lot because he'd been there many times before.

When we arrived at the woods he stood perfectly still until he was led to the area where he would be hooked to the ends of the logs. He had the patience of Job. My father cut the trees and we both peeled the bark off. Sometimes the bark didn't peel off easily, but other times it just fell away. A tool called a peavey was used to turn the tree and a spud was used to peel it, and by the end of the day the iron tool got very heavy. All through the day the commands "gee" and "haw" were all Old Kit needed to keep up his end of the work. After he had skidded a log, it was unhooked and without any commands he returned for another.

One morning when I was putting Old Kit's bridle on he moved forward in his stall and stepped on my foot. When he realized what he'd done he immediately pulled his leg up. My foot was just bruised and I was only laid up for a couple of days and then it was back to the wood lot.

Our dependence on horses has diminished over the years. Modern farm machinery, log trucks, pickup trucks, and cars have relieved us of the burdens of harnessing, training, and caring for the horse. As you drive through the North Country there are still horses pasturing in some places, but I would guess they are used more for pleasure than for work.

The Urge to Return

*A*fter graduating from high school in 1955, I filled a secretarial position in the County Attorney's office for a woman who was going on maternity leave. Along with my business subjects from high school, I had acquired some secretarial skills by the time the job was over.

In September, my Aunt Alice, who had formerly been a teacher in the small district school in Stowersville, agreed that I could come to Newburgh, a city in downstate New York, to live with her, her husband, John, and their three-year-old son, Tommy. Uncle John was originally from Tupper Lake, in the Adirondacks, and was a colonel in the United States Air Force. His assignment in Newburgh was to oversee a new communication system at the Stewart Air Force Base.

I finally got a job in a lawyer's office on Second Street in the heart of Newburgh. The office was extremely small, with no filing cabinets, and piles of papers on the desk and on chairs. My typewriter was in a very small, narrow room with no windows or ventilation. The eight-hour days seemed endless and I felt claustrophobic in the confined area.

I became very uncomfortable after stepping off the city bus that I took to get to my job. My upbringing in the Adirondacks had not prepared me for the congestion, paved city streets, tall buildings, noisy trucks, busses and cars, horns honking, and smelly exhaust fumes. People loitering under lampposts made me nervous. Some looked like they hadn't slept all night. Where I came from people always had a variety of jobs to do and there was no time for idleness. I thanked the Lord that I could go home to my aunt's beautiful house in the suburbs when the day's work was done.

One day my aunt asked me to take a ride with her. I've never forgotten it. Thomas E. Dewey, who served as governor of New York from 1943 to 1955, was standing at an outdoor podium, along with other officials. He was the main speaker and I actually saw the opening of the New York State Thruway.

Shortly after, I boarded a ferry to Beacon, New York, across the Hudson River from Newburgh, took a civil service test, and had an interview for a job at West Point. My uncle escorted me there and introduced me to top brass men in their executive offices, and we watched the cadets march.

Thankfully I didn't get the job because my aunt and uncle were transferred to another important assignment in Texas and I didn't want to stay alone in Newburgh.

I've been exposed to the worst and best of two worlds, the city life and the Adirondack life. In spite of some unhappy life experiences as I've grown older in this mountainous region, I have also experienced the serenity of the Adirondacks. The streets of Elizabethtown are safe to walk on and the beautiful change of seasons is something to look forward to.

Even though there has been progress, some things remain the same. The people are still very generous and friendly and there is always someone to turn to in time of trouble. Believe it or not, the neighbors still know one another and we all share a common bond that helps each one of us to exist.

Religion

$\mathcal{T}$he religious training I obtained as a child and teenager has brought me through many difficult trials in my life. During good weather we children were "dressed up" and attended church services in the Lewis Congregational Church.

The church sits on a hill in the center of the village of Lewis. It is one of the oldest Congregational churches in northeastern New York. Many steps lead from the main street to the church. They are lined with cedar trees. Like an umbrella the tree branches protect churchgoers from the rain until they come to the large portico attached to the front of the building.

Quite often when the church was filled to capacity, people were left standing under the portico. Of course, many people assembled when there was a death, a wedding, or a special service. Naturally, the portico also served as a place to share conversation with neighbors and friends.

Inside, a narrow hallway extends across most of the front of the church. Someone was usually there to greet you and usher you in. When I first stepped into the church my eyes always went directly to the stained glass window behind the altar. It portrays Jesus and a flock of sheep. Gently, He's holding a lamb in His arms and has a serene look on His face.

Always at that moment I realized that I was in the "House of God." Rays of sunshine came through the stained glass and illuminated the church. I always stood in awe for just a moment to experience a sense of well-being, strength, and peace.

Quietly my brother, sister, and I sat waiting with anticipation in our best Sunday clothes. The pews were covered with soft cushions, and hymn books and Bibles were on the backs of the seats. The organist and robed choir were in full view of the congregation. There are no words to describe the wholesome feelings when the organist began the church service with hymns such as "Rock of Ages" or "What a Friend We Have in Jesus."

Church services usually started at 11 a.m. It was a convenient time since it gave us a chance to do our daily chores. To begin, a welcoming address by the minister, a hymn, the sermon, and then more hymns helped the parents and children cope for another week.

There were all kinds of things to pray for—the families' health, money for expenses, good weather for haying, rain when the gardens wouldn't grow, and prosperity. Later on the church was a place of solace for the families who had been struck with polio. My brother was one of them. That was in the early 1950s when he was about eight years old.

Our family needed prayers as we watched him endure the pain and suffering. Several other people in the area were struck by the infectious disease. Some were left with permanent disabilities. Luckily, my brother wasn't paralyzed but he died of cancer at the young age of thirty-three.

The Congregational Church was a place to meditate about the mysteries of life. For one day each week Satan's evil spirits

My church

were pushed aside and life was perfect again, with a distinctive sense of renewal.

On a small, grassy slope in the Congregational Church cemetery my first baby, who was born with spina bifida, shares a plot of ground with my three brothers who died of cancer, my grandparents, aunts, and uncles, and many others who have left this world for their heavenly home.

After many years of service, the beams in the church have deteriorated and cracked. In 1990 the church council approved the trustees to begin a fund drive to raise money to restore the church. I hope others will find the consolation I often experienced while I attended the church and that the bells will continue to ring for them as well.

Life Today

𝓜y life today is as busy as it ever was, but in different ways. I especially enjoy the company of my four grown children and three grandchildren, ages ten, seven, and one. I well remember a time without a telephone, but am so grateful to be able to have a quick conversation with my relatives and friends by just putting a receiver to my ear.

So far, I haven't had the opportunity to travel much, but I was a docent at the Rockwell Kent and Myers museums at Plattsburgh State University. I was a part of a group that traveled to the Museum of Fine Arts in Boston. It was an extremely rewarding experience since I've always been interested in art. When I retire I would like to visit friends in Connecticut and Florida and see other scenery.

In the fall of 1994, family members gathered to pay their last respects to my eighty-two-year-old father, who had always lived in the Adirondacks. Besides being a father, he was an Adirondack logger and storeowner and he served his community throughout his lifetime.

My father taught us to endure and persevere. He always found a way when times were tough. He lived and raised a family through Depression years and taught me that there's always a way. He knew that hard work and sharing would get us through the hard times.

Recently I've had the opportunity to share my mother's old photos with her. One day she brought out a box of black-and-white and tintype photos that were wrapped in an old head scarf. We spent a good deal of time looking over her special photographs of people from the late 1800s and on up. I found one particular aunt of hers who looked exactly like me and I was happy to see the likeness.

I like to cook, oil paint, and take pictures. I also enjoy writing and want to become more active in some of the community organizations. Unlike many places in the United States, our small village of Elizabethtown still seems safe and provides nice streets to walk on. Since I love to walk, it's the ideal place to enjoy the beautiful surroundings and stop and visit with a neighbor.

In addition, our writing group has given me an opportunity to express myself and share my life experiences with others. I've enjoyed the company of Melba Wrisley, Sadie Cantin, Marilyn Cross, and Joan Potter. We've shared dinner, done readings, and had quiet, interesting chats at each other's homes with refreshments to boot.

In spite of a few shortcomings, I'm a very happy Adirondacker.

Picture Credits

All the photographs in this book appear through the interest and generosity of the following people:

Sonja Aubin
Sadie Cantin
Marilyn Cross
Conrad Hutchins
Reid Larson, Essex County Historical Society
Al Reiner
Melba Wrisley

Map of the Elizabethtown/Lewis area by Elayne Sears